ENCHANTMENT

Do you ask your shadow what became of it
during the night?
Or ask the night about your shadow?

—Edmond Jabès, *The Book of Questions*

ENCHANTMENT

Stories by
DORIS VALLEJO
Illustrated by
BORIS VALLEJO

THUNDER'S MOUTH PRESS
NEW YORK

Thunder's Mouth Press
632 Broadway
Seventh Floor
New York, NY 10012

First published 1985
First Thunder's Mouth Press Edition 1996

Originally published in the United States by Ballantine Books,
a division of Random House, Inc., New York

Text design by Alex Jay/Studio J

Library of Congress Card Catalog Number: 96-61956
ISBN 1-56025-120-4

Distributed by Publishers Group West
4065 Hollis Street
Emeryville, CA 94608

Printed in Singapore.

CONTENTS

SEDUCTION

A vampire came into the bedroom one night. I awoke to find her lying between us. The air had been oppressive in the house. We'd left the window open, never thinking this might be interpreted as an invitation. Both the vampire and my husband appeared to be sleeping. Has she killed him, I wondered. I felt no terror. Without knowing for certain, I sensed that he must still be alive.

Had the vampire first been attracted to him or to me? I suppose I shall never know. If I ask her, I cannot assume she will tell me the truth. I got out of bed and sat in a chair to better assess the situation. They lay motionless in each other's arms, their eyes closed, their lips parted as though for a kiss.

I have always felt certain of my husband's love. Though his work as a photographer brings him into contact with many beautiful women, I have never suffered even the slightest prickle of jealousy. The failed love affairs or dissolving marriages of people we know always made him wistful. "I want to spend the rest of my life with you," he would say.

A gleam, sharp as a hiss in her silent mouth, limned two silvery fangs. My hand went involuntarily to my throat. The area was slightly tender. I perceived two infinitesimal puncture wounds. This comforted me strangely. I thought, she may be sleeping with her arms around him but it was me she wanted first. I seemed to remember the path of her lips and the rush of pleasure they evoked.

Their faces, illuminated by moonlight, might have been chiseled out of mother of pearl; exquisite sculptures. Should I lie down again beside them?

I decided against it.

The atmosphere was charged with a queer tension. Her black cape lay across the foot of the bed and I had the impression that a gargoyle, grinning hideously from its folds, was seeking to draw me into some sinister collusion. Imagination— nothing more, I told myself. There is no gargoyle in the cape.

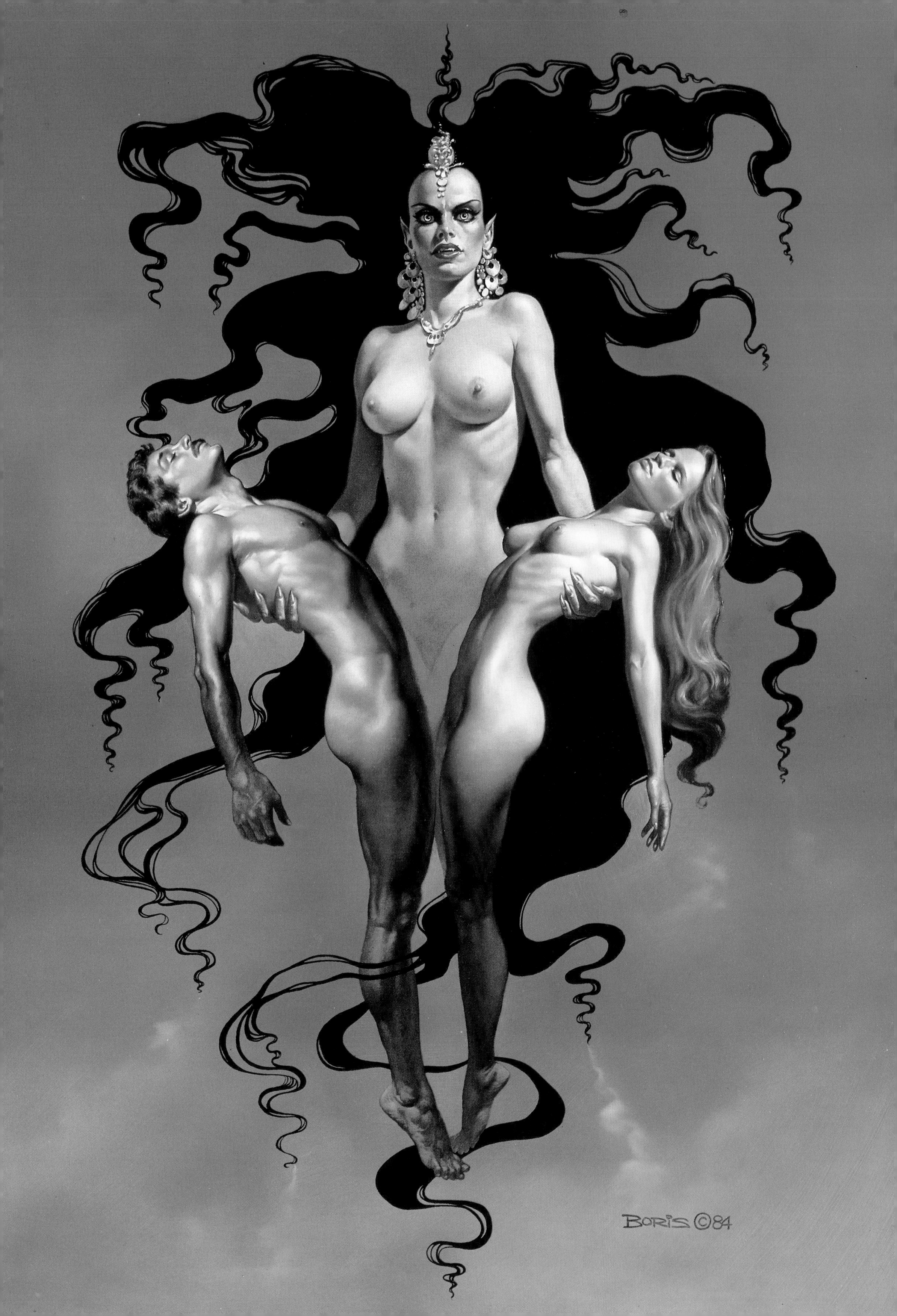
BORIS ©84

Her beautiful hair flowed like a dark halo around her head. Part of my husband's face was hidden in that halo. The part I could still see—kind, strong featured—seemed to be smiling. She wore a mist-thin gown through which her nipples showed, hard as marbles.

She is asleep, I told myself. This is the moment I must make use of. This is the moment, as vampire legends dictate, that I must plunge a wooden stake into her heart. Yet I did not. Her superb body was too solid, too real. Besides, I had no wooden stake. And she was not really asleep.

She rose suddenly, retrieved her cape, and glided across the room with the soundless grace of a jungle cat. I was struck by her lithe elegance, her beauty, the mysterious electricity that flowed from her like a siren song. She drew the cape around her shoulders and fastened it at her neck. Her mouth, with its startling glint of fangs, was hidden by the high collar as her eyes were masked by darkness. I couldn't tell if she had divined my only half-serious impulse to murder her. Or even who she was looking at, my husband or me.

Standing near the window in her long black cape (so reminiscent of another era), she might have been a friend on the way to a masquerade. She might have been calling for me, waiting for me to put on my own costume, perhaps waiting to help me fasten the difficult to reach snaps in the back. Or else she might have been waiting for me to rise, to push the thin lace straps of my nightgown off my shoulders, to let it drop to the floor, to step out of it, to lie back naked against the pillows, to open my arms to her, to bare my throat . . .

At the window she was no more than a silhouette against the somber houses and the night-bright sky. I meant to say something, to ask her something. My husband awoke and, sitting up slowly, looked from me to her as if aware of my need. I thought he would ask the question that refused to take shape on my own tongue. I waited. The silhouette dissolved into a swiftly dissipating black vapor, and a small creature flew away on leathery wings.

When the rapid flapping had receded into silence, I went to the window. My husband joined me. There was no more trace of the creature. I might have conjured her out of my subconscious, given breadth and depth to her out of no more than elemental dreams and fears. But my husband spoke of her, pondered the sundry ramifications of an *affaire* such as we were offered, conjectured that it would broaden our love for each other, and (perhaps to erase a persistent foreboding) embraced me and impassionately kissed the injured place on my neck. Thus unburdened of

apprehensions, we returned to bed. He put his arms around me and I fell asleep at once.

All day we were preoccupied by thoughts of our vampire: would she come? when? what hour? what minute? Yet we spoke of her to no one, and to each other only with glances. The memory of her was an exhilarating secret that gave us a sense of conspiracy, of heightened living. Only *we* shared her sanguine caresses.

That night a recently divorced friend of ours called. He expressed much pessimism about adjusting to bachelor life and invited us for dinner and to help him stave off the blues. My husband told him we'd already eaten and had made other plans for the evening. An obvious lie. He knew we never ate that early and rarely went out during the week. Undoubtedly he was hurt. Should we call him back? Claim a last-minute change? Say we were free to see him after all?

No. Things happened as they were meant to happen.

My husband suggested that we take a bath together, make a celebration out of bathing, a prelude, so to speak, to the restlessly anticipated rendezvous. We drank champagne out of long-stemmed glasses and luxuriated in the jasmine-scented water.

Afterwards I brushed my hair until it fell in long, shining waves and put on a sheer white negligee through which my nipples and pubic area appeared provocatively dark. My husband, eschewing pajamas (which he considered unnecessary for sleep and a hindrance to lovemaking), put on a blue light knit robe I once made for him. He drew back the bedroom curtains and opened the window.

We sat and waited in the semidarkness.

"If she comes, fine," he said after a while. "If she doesn't come, also fine."

I agreed, thinking, nevertheless, But she has to come.

An hour passed. Another hour. He took off his robe. We lay down. He began to stroke me. First my shoulders and arms and breasts, then my legs and between my legs. I turned to him sliding one leg across both of his. Over his shoulder I saw a movement in the corner by the bureau: a face, malevolent and terrifying. I must have involuntarily tensed.

"What is it?" he asked me.

But it was only the shifting light pattern on the wall made by clouds drifting ceaselessly across the moon. All at once they were blotted out.

For a moment she perched on the windowsill, large, much larger than I remembered her, filling the window, shutting out the moon and the starlight entirely. It became intensely black in the room, the air thick, stifling, impossible to breathe.

Then she was beside us, the moonlight dancing

around her like fireflies. I reached out to her. She embraced me, remolding my body against the curves and hollows of her own. Breathing became possible again. It almost seemed I breathed her in, so completely did she enter me. The sweet intoxicating venom of her being affected me like an opiate.

"Can one become addicted to kisses?" I murmured into the softness of her hair. Her moving weight on me, the feel of her body through the silk-film of her gown, her hands: tender, almost unbearably so, and, at the same time, wounding, annihilating...

I knew perfectly well what would happen next. Yet I was not in the least frightened nor did I cringe from the stab-shock of her fangs at my throat. Rather, my blood panted warmly against them as they sank easily and (so I thought) lovingly deep into the vein.

The pain was momentary, lasting only for that fraction of time it took to pierce the skin. A gradually increasing warmth spread through me. Then a heat, a burning roared through me with such violence I was sure the blood she drew must blister her mouth, must sear a gory path into her like bubbling lava. This idea aroused me even more. I wound my arms and legs about her and strove, quite beside myself, to drive her into me, to become fused, to become one with her.

From a great distance I felt my husband's hands, his tongue hard and wet along my spine and between my buttocks, as if it were not me he caressed. Or rather, as if I were not me. And then she turned to him and it was I who, treading the sheets for closeness, kissed, licked, grasped at them across the vastness of the bed.

When she arose to leave, I noticed that blood (his? mine?) had stained her lips. I found this oddly beautiful, as though she had feasted on roses and the surfeit, the two sweet petals that had been in excess, now clung delicately to the corners of her mouth.

It was not with total naiveté that we entered into this liaison. We did not pretend to ourselves or to each other that there was no danger. Priding ourselves on our circumspection, we stayed awake after she left, to await the sunrise. If the light caused pain, we reasoned, it would mean that we must not see her again; that we must uproot her from our fantasies; that we must shut our windows as well as ourselves ruthlessly against her.

A murky fog obscured the street. It rose with the first pale hint of light and hung grayly on the rooftops of the taller houses. With the warm, confident rising of the sun, it magically vanished. No curlicue of slime remained looped over a chimney as a ghostly reminder. The strain and pallor faded from my husband's face. I too found the morning light remarkably revitalizing. We are still safe, we assured each other.

Thus it became our habit, after each of her visits, to await the sunrise. And only then, after having anxiously determined that we were safe for yet another day, to sleep for a few hours. The effects of all this were subtle, hardly noticeable at first.

"I love you," my husband began to tell me more and more often—as if by repetition to confirm what might otherwise be in question. And he often seemed to be absent in thought only to return abruptly, his eyes glazed with an unnatural sheen, and demand to know what *I* was thinking of, then, right that minute.

I appeared unchanged to myself. But I cannot say for sure that these new and disquieting traits of his were not prompted by some alteration in me. Eventually one or another of our acquaintances would inquire if everything was all right. We looked worn, they would say. We had both lost weight. Did we feel all right? Should we, perhaps, see a doctor?

At first we merely disregarded what we felt to be officious concern. Later I (if not my husband) began to wonder. We'd both developed such dark hollows around the eyes. Of course that might be perfectly natural, considering how little sleep we got by on those days. There was no obvious reason to be concerned.

Our nights were not always spent in the tempestuous blood-lathered embraces that I described earlier. These episodes, no matter how momentarily exhilarating, always left me listless and depressed and my husband curiously agitated. It was as if, complete and whole during our lovemaking, we became alarmingly fragmented at its conclusion.

Our vampire would have to cajole, to court, to win us anew—which she could do quite charmingly. She could change into a beautiful glossy cat and, purring, rub herself against our legs. Or she could change into a sable fox with a moist black snout and a long fluffy tail, and stalk the mingling moonlight and shadows that formed and transformed our bedroom world. She could change into a hypnotically coiling snake, rainbow colored, satin skinned, and with a swiftly flicking tongue that promised to spark irresistible delights. She could change into a huge fantastic bird, half eagle, half peacock.

I think this was my favorite of her transformations, particularly when I was the one to climb on her back and fly over the city with her. When it was my husband she chose to fly with—which meant that I would spend the subsequent hours with only the vast, receptive night as my lover—my enchantment with the bird considerably dimmed.

Curiously enough, though I am fearful of plane trips and heights in general, I was never afraid of falling during these flights with her. With my legs tight against her rounded plumy sides and my hands buried in the ruffling feathers near her wings, I felt invulnerable. I was surprised that no one noticed us as we dipped through the streets and rose up past the windows.

"Are we invisible?" I shouted to her.

Her answer whirled past me in the surging wind.

Once it happened that we went so far it was just getting light as we returned.

"I thought vampires were afraid of the daylight," I said.

"A superstition," she answered.

"You mean I couldn't destroy you by keeping you out till dawn," I said teasingly, not really expecting an answer.

Her crested head turned toward me, her eyes indis-
nething about her
vhat I took to be a

the city. We saw a
, untie the sash of
o reveal her full,
. Taking his hand,
d began to stroke
; which had been

on top of herself.
ough water, they
erged, rising and
-kiss of the wind.
e us? Their eyes
wasn't possible.
satiated? Happy?

two men, writh-
swimmer strug-
r air: *yes...yes...*
caping, gurgling
The man affixed
ling, devouring,
man at her back
d... tell me... tell

rea of tenements
ll of threadbare
ngaged in what
. They advanced,
in agility in their
artner between
ar-hug embrace
egan pounding,
cry came. A knife
saber tooth of a
very fangs of the

With the appearance of the knife a strange excitement, a heightened alertness swept through the vampire's bird body. Still mounted on her back, I could feel the accelerated beating of her heart on my bare thighs and bottom.

Invisible, we watched the dance, the staccato drumbeats of our own hearts so much faster than the thrusts and parries of the dancers that I wondered if we could endure to the end; that I wondered how long I could hold my breath, which finally escaped in a rasping groan as the dance came to a tottering end.

The knife handle jutted from between the man's ribs. His blood spouted like spring water onto the yellow-flecked linoleum. We waited for the woman to run from the room before we entered and the vampire slaked, somewhat, her endless thirst.

The wounded man's breath came so lightly, so shallowly, it was impossible to tell when, exactly, it stopped. His eyes, like those of the red-haired woman and the boy, remained open, staring, an expression of abstract amazement in them.

"I wish you wouldn't be gone so long," my husband said when we returned as the sun was already clear of the horizon. "You might think of me a little. You might have the insight to realize that I would be worried."

"About which of us were you concerned?" I asked.

"About both of you," he answered.

But I wondered. On those nights when he went flying with her, it was resentment, not worry, that stirred my heart. I nurtured what I knew to be a childish possessiveness: the suspicion that they preferred each other to me.

The nights turned cold. We no longer left the bedroom window open. Instead we sat there waiting so that when our vampire came we might open it to admit her and close it at once. The waiting wore us out. And our conversations while we waited invariably fixated on the same themes: When was she coming? (Sometimes it was well past midnight.) Was she coming at all? What if we were never to see her again? That would be a relief in a way—wouldn't it? A relief from the waiting, the not knowing... a relief from the tide of jealousies that had insidiously risen around us. A relief from the hunger for reassurances—*Yes I love you, yes I love you best, yes I'll love you always, yes and again yes, yes...* that were never enough to bolster a gradually diminishing trust.

"I resent this eternal waiting," my husband would say. "Maybe we shouldn't wait. Maybe we just shouldn't be there when she comes."

I'd agree with him and, at the same time, would think how our lives would be distinctly emptier without her: no more of the fantastic night trips over the city, no more of the phantasmal games in which we streamed through one anothers veins, pumped by the same orgastic force.

"Vampires sleep in coffins," I would say. "If we could just find out where hers is... If we could go there in the daytime and open it then..."

"No," my husband always said. "That would be a betrayal, an invasion."

"An invasion of unhallow ground. Who'd condemn that?"

"I can't do it. Besides, she may not sleep in a coffin. She doesn't seem particularly bound by the usual vampire conventions."

"What about garlic? Or a cross? A cross might work against her. Have you noticed that she seems to avoid churches and the like?"

In the end we always waited and she always appeared. Something inside me, like the delicate fluttering of a moth's wings, would be stilled with her coming. I am dying, I would think, and push the thought away.

Unhappiness is fatiguing. One day, more tired, more wretched than before, I saw betrayal as the only means of salvation. Would our marriage survive it? That no longer seemed to matter. I bought a white ivory cross on a gold chain, which I concealed under my clothes. Thus I took the first unretractable step.

When she came, unsuspecting (though I wonder in retrospect how that could have been, since she was uncannily perceptive about our moods and our thoughts), I retreated to the center of the room, letting my husband open the window for her and greet her alone. She gave him only a cursory nod and came toward me, her inscrutable face mesmerizingly beautiful. I loved her with all the unbearable passion of the suicidal for death and it was only with the crazed strength of despair that I pulled my robe open to reveal the white cross. It began to burn on my chest. She saw it, froze, and at that moment a dazzling explosion sent thin brilliant needles of light into my dilated pupils.

When I could see again, I found that she seemed neither alarmed nor especially surprised. She had not moved. Behind her, my husband had gone ashen with horror, as if I stood suddenly revealed to him as a stranger, an enemy. *Had we only possessed, at the beginning, the circumspection of hindsight.* A bewildering emptiness swelled within me. I breathed his name.

The world receded. I saw the grinning mask that had been our vampire's face grow transparent. I saw the depthlessness it had hidden. I saw the faintly stirring curtains of our window through it. And through it I also saw, beyond the window, the unimaginably distant stars.

I came to on the floor. The room was unbearably cold, the window open to the night. The curtains slapped against it as if with the passage and repassage of unseen creatures. I closed the window and locked it and drew the curtains firmly across it. I went to where my husband lay. His face, more aged and drawn than I had realized, kindled a poignant remorse. I almost wondered who he was. Then I got blankets and covered him where he lay.

Alone in our bed, shivering under the quilt, I couldn't shake the numbness that had fastened itself to me.

In the morning, the room was warmer.

We have not seen the vampire again. We take certain precautions. We do not go out at night. We keep the windows locked and the curtains drawn, not just in the bedroom, in all the rooms. And we always keep the lights burning to dispel the dark.

Still, the memory of her casts palpable shadows, oppressive as a lingering sense of guilt. Her return (or that of someone like her), which we now dread, seems inevitable. We don't speak of it. We try not to think of it. During the day we keep busy with our work. At night we watch TV, absorbing the din of news reports and the trivial chatter of game shows. Sometimes we listen to music—loud barbarous music that numbs the eardrums as well as the brain. And we view the encroaching sunsets with sand-dry eyes.

WEB

Does A enjoy being tied to the bed? Is she aware of the strong visual impact of her tanned body spread-eagled against snow-white sheets? Or is she furious? Is it with fury that she squirms, twists, bucks her hips against his mouth in sharp jabs as he crouches between her legs? He can do anything he wants to her right now and there is no way she can stop him. Unless she gets loose. He has tied her wrists and ankles tightly. Still, she is lithe, quick, powerful as a tigress. She might conceivably slip the bonds.

He loves her firm athletic body in which the softly curving belly is almost a contradiction. He loves her alert, glittering eyes and her small, sharp teeth. They lend her face an intriguing savagery.

In some ways she is savage, her lovemaking often tantamount to outright attack from which he wears the resulting teeth marks and bruises as if they were stripes earned for bravery. Unlike other women he knew, she never needed to be coaxed into making love. She was always eager. Immediately afterwards, however, she would retreat into herself as though they were not still lying together. As though they were not even in the same room together. He would see in her a strange feral creature callously inspecting him, waiting...

On impulse he once asked her if she considered men to be her enemies. They had been lying at opposite ends of the bed. In response she reached out, took his flaccid organ in her hand, and, giving it short, hard squeezes (that despite a certain discomfort caused it to waken), crooned: "This my enemy? This plump delicious juicy love?"

He tests the silk ropes that cut into her ankles and wrists; jerks at them to make sure they won't give.

"You think I can't get free?" Her face is enigmatic. No telling what is going on behind that thin smile.

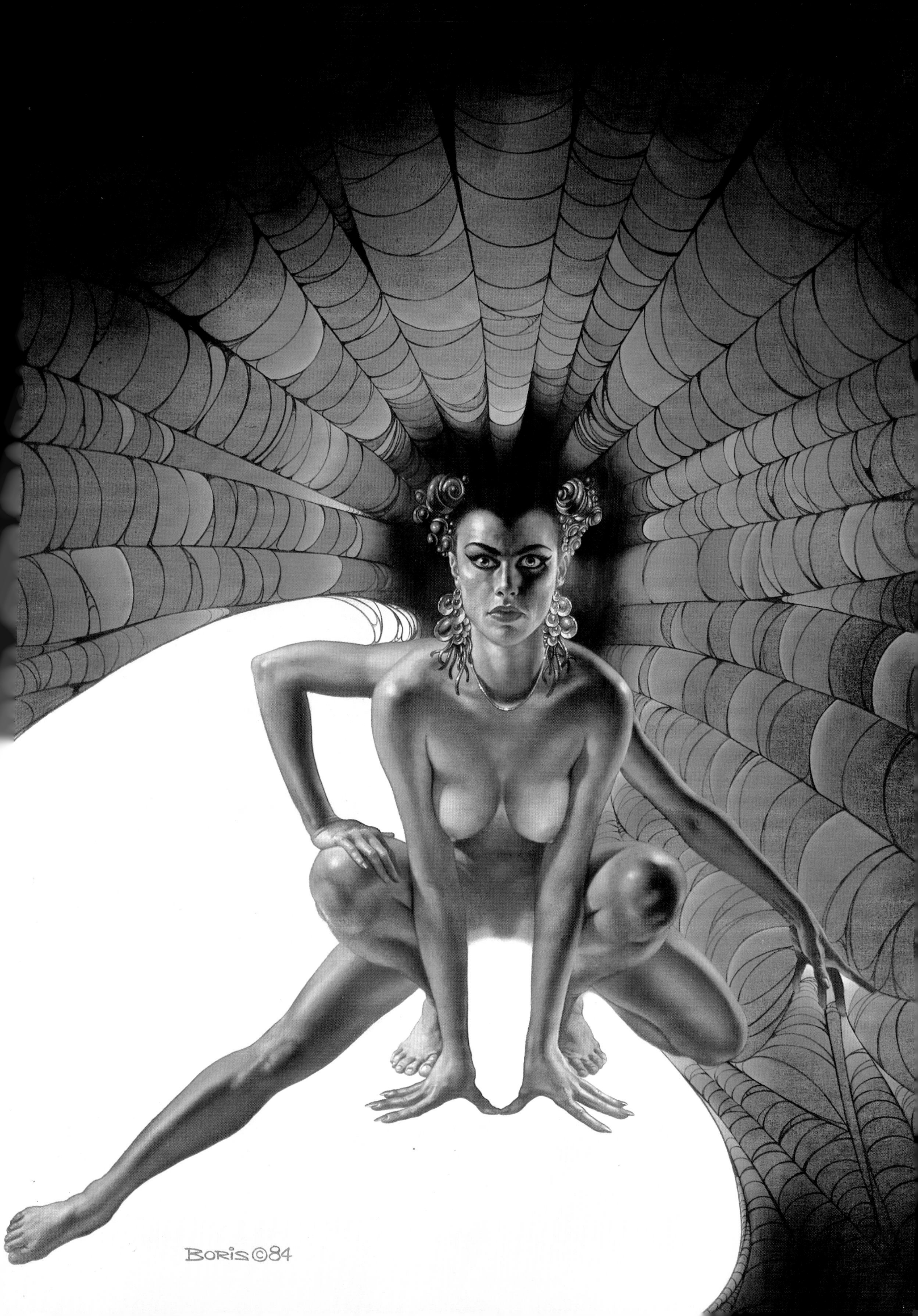
BORIS ©84

"Of course you can if I let you." He strokes the soles of her feet, her toes, runs his fingers lightly over the silk knots and along her legs, plays his fingers against the grain of the fine pale hairs of her inner thighs, and, without warning, shoots his hand upward, up, all the way home.

She is dark and mellow and welcoming. She is diamond hard and ferocious: a razor-edged jewel. He is an adventurer, a daredevil; he is a madman leaping chasms, bellowing victory, running riot with glorious intoxicating strength.

I believe M does little or nothing in my absence. As though he has no life away from me. The other day, when I came back into the bedroom after washing myself, he was still lying on the bed as I had left him. He looked horribly thin. His ribs showed in bas relief under that ashen skin, which was patterned with scratches (some of them still bloody).

"Look at you," I said. "You are a pig. At least you could go and clean yourself up instead of getting stains all over the sheets."

Rather than move, he gave me an injured look. Wholly transparent, this attempt to put me in the wrong. I paid no attention.

Admittedly, I am phobic about bloodstains on the sheets. The sight of them can drive me into a frenzy.

"They can't hurt you," M has said. Which is true enough, but doesn't make any difference. M claims my phobia is simply affectation. I prefer to write it off as a human peculiarity. We all have peculiarities. At least M, to his credit, doesn't argue that.

The other day, as if it were the most remarkable discovery, he insisted I come to see a small whitish spider spinning its web in the corner of our bedroom window. It was a perfectly ordinary spider spinning a perfectly ordinary web and I found his enthusiasm a bit irksome. This web, more like coarse sacking than a lace-fine snare, lacked subtlety, in my opinion.

Characteristically, M disagreed, which he does, I suspect, for the sheer, stupid joy of being contentious.

"It's wonderfully suited to its purpose," he said. "No self-respecting insect would be attracted to a few flimsy threads wafting in the breeze." His theory, preposterous as usual, was that insects were drawn by the web, actually seduced by the lovely, shining network of silk that, from the very beginning, they sensed was a trap. They deliberately courted terror, according to him. Terror gave them weight. As if the rush of its searing reality through their tiny bodies was what kept them from floating to life's surface like so many dead fish.

He might have known that this theorizing would annoy me.

He has a talent for setting me on edge. This morning, for instance. Of course I was still angry with him for what happened last night, so, to begin with, I tried to ignore him.

"You take advantage of me," he whined after a while. "I adore you and your thanks are to treat me like shit."

I burst out laughing, although, heaven knows, there was nothing humorous in this remark. He immediately assumed his whipped-dog pose: head lowered, tail limp between the legs, eyes mournfully large. I felt like telling him to cut it out; that I, for one, did not confuse this gutless suffering of his with love. And even if it was love, I would prefer to be hated fairly and squarely rather than subjected to this sickening, chancrous passion. However, I kept my mouth shut. The most irrefutable logic is lost on M if he feels himself criticized. The most civilized discussion abruptly turns vicious. Not ready to let myself in for that mess, I took my car keys and left.

"When will you be back?" he called down the stairs.

"When you see me," I shouted up.

He didn't ask where I was going. I should have known that he intended to follow me.

A is great in the throes of her moments: flinging herself about, rolling, arching against him, emitting those tremulous little cries that rise to a heart-stopping crescendo. This splended delirium to which he can drive her, this unequivocal proof of his mastery, is, largely, what binds him to her. Let other men belly-ache about their women's indifference. She is proof of his exceptional prowess.

I should let her go, he had thought, racing after her blue Porsche in his decrepit rattling Lynx. All day she'd been fermenting a row (the premenstrual black and blues?), which he'd diplomatically sought to avoid, and now this: tearing like lunatics along Route 134 in the dead of the night.

I should damn well let her go to hell, he thought. The bulwark of trees had unsheathed a narrow, twisting road; alive and dark, it shot toward him and snaked between the wheels of his car. He spun around a hairpin bend, and his headlights caught the gleam of eyes just ahead. He braked, propelling the car into a shrieking skid though they were hardly evil-spirit eyes, only those of little wild creatures. Raccoons or groundhogs. At least he didn't hit any of them. They fled into the sanctuary of the night and he sped on after her.

Baleful shapes shuddered in his rearview mirror: the suggestion that something stalked him, hungered for him, squatted there in the back seat of his car awaiting only his slackened attention to spring, to seize him, to dart its flesh-dissolving venom into him, to consumate some fatal intimacy. Of course there was nothing there. The back seat was empty. Of course.

And why was he chasing her? Why the hell didn't he just turn around and go back while he was still *compos mentis* and in one piece?

The road widened unexpectedly. The densely growing trees withdrew there where a solitary street lamp burned like a full moon anchored to the earth. Her Porsche stood beside it. She sat slumped behind the wheel.

A wave of tenderness swept him. How could he leave her? What would she do without him? She would be lost. Like now, for instance: she had probably run out of gas.

His spike thudding inside me . . .

The sneak. He thinks it's so clever to have tied me down. Silk knots can be slipped in seconds. He should know . . .

Still . . .

His heaviness, his succulent smell, his hands . . . Why should I spoil this for myself. I can wait. M, you little love worm, you weevil, you do feel good.

And it's only or mainly your accusing silences that get to me, your sitting crumpled up in a corner and, when I ask you what it's all about, your answering with a non-answer: *Oh, nothing,* or, *Nothing important,* or, *I don't know.* Have you any idea how insulting that is? Sometimes I suspect those moods, those non-answers are meant to be taunting: a weighing and balancing act to see how far you can go before I strike

back. But what's the use of telling you this. You counter every legitimate complaint of mine with silences, with sadness, with your infuriating martyrdom.

So I wanted to get the hell away from you earlier, and why not? Scrawny as you've become, you were still too big to be kicked out of your retreat, your crumple in the corner. Your tide of crocodile tears was still too strong for me to stem. The alternative would have been to scream insults at you, to kick you in the shins, to punch and scratch you, and, eventually, to rock you in my arms and kiss the wounds I'd inflicted. And to wonder at the strangling anger that tightened in my chest like a cramp.

So I left to avoid all that which was otherwise inevitable, as we both ought to know. Haven't we played the scene over and over, repeating each move and countermove as if in rehearsal for some final definitive act? It is always the same, M. And you always pretend that I have fluffed my lines, although I speak perfectly distinctly and no one else would have trouble understanding what I say. The whole awful scene at the party last night would have been avoided if only you'd stayed near me when the lights went off.

It was obviously just someone's drunken idea of a joke, because they went back on almost immediately and everyone was still masked. Only, I'd had enough. I was getting feverish under that rubber face you had me wear, so I took it off. I would have liked to leave at that point but I couldn't find you anywhere—annoying enough in itself since I don't care for large parties and only came because of you. Naturally, I could have left without you, but I would have had to endure your reproaches for days. You had just been beside me and I couldn't imagine how you'd managed to disappear so quickly.

You tell me I isolate you. With my selfish insistence on privacy and what you call my contemptuous attitude toward your friends, I prevent you from enjoying a more social life. You refuse to understand how I can be happier in their absence, how I can say that social encounters are no more than performances. You reject any possibility of finding comfort in solitude and blame your frequent lows on loneliness. It was for your sake, your happiness, that I agreed to go to this party, although *agreed* is hardly the word for it. *Begged* is more accurate. It is perverse that I had to beg you to go, considering our viewpoints on the subject. And you offered such transparent objections: *We have no costumes, nothing interesting to wear. I'd rather forget it than go in some ordinary five-and-dime getup. We'll just forget it, that's what.*

Suppose I had taken you up on that? Don't tell me you wouldn't have moped for weeks. Predictably, you allowed me to convince you. And then, those costumes.... Were you so inspired by that puny spider spinning a web at the window that you considered no other disguises than spider and fly? Oh, you looked fine enough in your dark gray leotard and tights, your mask made of glitter, and your rainbow-tinted wings. But I would have preferred something more attractive than black drapery, a black rubber gargoyle face, and eight bent wires (that no one would mistake for legs) jutting from my sides. How did you imagine I'd enjoy maneuvering through that heaving crush of bodies with those wiggling antennae?

People were dancing although there was hardly any room for this. They were banging into each other. Because they all still wore their masks, I recognized no one. A great deal of laughter spewed out from behind those immobile faces. The noise, the heat, the intensifying odor of sweat, together with my frustration at not being able to find you...

The floor seemed to tilt from side to side. I felt nauseous. I lost my balance and fell against a fat man in a snapping turtle suit. I excused myself as pleasantly as I could, but I think he misinterpreted this. He was clutching a six-pack of beer under one arm. He reached for me with his free hand and hissed something that ended with the word *fuck*.

"Fuck yourself," I yelled at him and dodged his grasp.

And where were you, my sweet? my insouciant M? On the floor at the far far end of the room nuzzling a woman dressed as a boa constrictor—an apt disguise, I might add, since she was wound around you in what looked like a terminal clinch. But you were drunk and, being drunk (you claim), quite innocent in mistaking her for me. That you didn't recognize me when I began pulling at you ought to confirm this—you claim.

What I would like to know is how you got that drunk in a matter of minutes. And how you forgot—when you designed the costume yourself—that I was a spider and not a snake. Short curcuit in the gray matter? That sort of thing is known to happen, particularly when guzzling tequila with lemons. (And it is true that I found several chewed lemon rinds scattered around you two.) It is true that you looked up at my unmasked face (which is the face that people love or hate me by and which was, no doubt, sweaty and flushed) without any recognition whatsoever so that for a moment I actually wondered if it was I who had made the mistake. But I'd know you in any costume, behind any mask. I'd know you with my eyes closed. In the darkness. At a distance of two hundred feet. That panicky tempo of your pulse is all too familiar.

There you were on the floor, your beautiful wings crushed. There you were, grappling, drooling, moaning in that suffocating embrace. Tell me, just to satisfy my curiosity, does slow suffocation intensify the pleasure? I've heard that the reduction of oxygen to the brain can play tantalizing tricks with the cock and I've always wondered. But your answers—*I swear to you I didn't realize... I didn't mean... I didn't want—I would never...* —were not too enlightening.

Were you, behind your piteous apologies, blaming me? That you bought me a bouquet of paper flowers was touching, I admit. It was just not enough to patch everything up. And that's why, when you asked me why I didn't put them in water, I told you it was because they were already dead. I did not intend that as a cue for you to lie sullenly in bed and brood all the long afternoon. Or to accuse me, in your mournful voice, of hating you—which I denied, apparently without sufficient conviction. But you can be maddening with or without my prompting.

"Hatred is worth more than love," you told me, "since love is nothing more than the need to possess. Love is nothing more than the need to fuse with the love object. It connotes nothing nobler than the surrender of self; a kind of bondage."

"Come off it," I said. "So you didn't realize the flowers were made of paper. Big deal."

This method of humoring you fell flat.

"Love is frustration," you said, "because one plus one always and invariably equals two."

So I brought you an ice pack for your head and massaged your neck and back for a while.

He is rain: driving, flattening against me. His cock is a sapling swelling from the moist earth. We meet, merge, mutate into a single being and he is wholly wrong about one plus one, which can equal anything, anything at all. Out of the corner of my eye (which is also his) I watch his belly pumping against me, and his tongue stroking sweetly, and I have long ago slipped through the slip knots, which he has not noticed...

His breath cries into my ears, a waxing waning lullaby. He curls into me, a caterpillar into its chrysalis. His blood thrumming through my veins announces: *Soon... soon... soon...*

Without him A would be lost. Hasn't she said so? Haven't they both agreed on this many times?

"I would be nothing without you. A shadow. Less than a shadow." He remembers her saying this over and over as if in a recurrent dream.

In a way she is his creation, truly, as the dream is the creation of the dreamer. Though she faults him for his seeming lack of ambition, she fails to consider that he is a creator. Realities that did not exist once were born through him. Once she was no more than a shadow fluttering against the night and he made her real, beautiful, desirable, fierce.

Designing the spider costume for her had been an incredible experience. After hours of blankness, no ideas at all, inspiration had suddenly shaken him through and through. He'd showered and shaved, put on fresh underwear and a clean shirt, lit a cigarette (to steady his nerves), and sitting down at his little desk, had finally begun, anxiously, lovingly, to draw the robe, the veils, the eight spindle legs graceful as reeds.

How he regretted the ridiculous incident that had taken on the aspects of a nightmare. A misunderstanding. And for endless hours she tortured him over it, refusing to speak, ignoring him, making him feel ugly, dirty, worthless. As if the hangover he had to endure was not punishment enough.

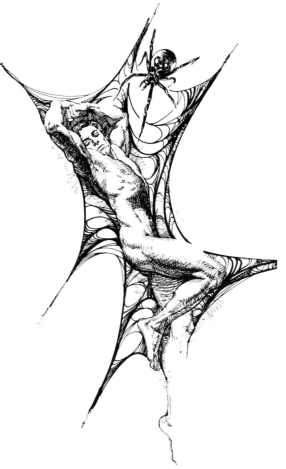

In fact the real culprit was the brandy someone had thrust into his hand in the dark. Of course he should have remembered that he couldn't handle brandy. Gin, yes. Rum, yes. But one brandy and he was no longer responsible for what he might do. A year ago, after knocking back two small cognacs, he'd spent an hour roaming the same block in search of his house and another hour trying to hold the damn keyhole in place so he could unlock the door.

How should he have known that she'd removed her mask? He wasn't a mind reader. And she blamed him for that. She played the injured party while he was in agony. She bustled importantly back and forth while the minutes of his life waggled by like so many sheep. She made him feel like dirt while he loved her, while inwardly he howled for her like a newborn baby deprived of milk.

Whose fault was it that, because he'd been temporarily blinded when the lights went back on, he didn't, *for one miniscule instant*, recognize her unmasked? She had leaped at him, screamed at him, awesome in her fury, her little teeth glittering, her eyes wide and terrible. Oh, she had scared him all right. She had made him nearly sick with fright. Still, he was smarter than she gave him credit for. Talking calmly, reassuringly, he bided his time until he got her off guard.

So, when she stretched out wholly naked on the bed and rubbed her eyes, he had asked, casually, if she would like him to rub her neck and her back and so on. She agreed readily and without the slightest suspicion of the ghosts gathering beneath his skin like a vengeful mob. After a while he asked her to turn around so he could rub her her feet. She loved this because, as she told him, it was so wonderfully relaxing. All that time he had the silk ropes ready, and when she seemed on the verge of falling asleep, he looped those fine nooses around her wrists and ankles, pulled them tight, and fastened them in the same movement. And so, magically, their roles had been reversed.

Slowly, pleasurably, he bore down on her as she struggled. Now it was she who trembled. He could feel her trembling through his thighs and pelvis and most of all through his cock. It was overwhelming, the exquisite delicacy of the feeling that arose out of what was, in actuality, a kind of rape.

But she is loose, suddenly, clawing at him, vicious. She tears his flesh. He is frozen. Mesmerized. And she is all over him, biting him on the face, punching, kicking. She has gone suddenly murderously berserk: flaying him with her bare hands, choking him, breaking his ribs, and being, at the same time, terrifyingly, voraciously loving—nosing, lapping, sucking at his wounds.

He cries out to her to stop but she doesn't understand and straddles him, pins him down, traps him beneath her strong shiny body that is all arms and legs and furious devouring mouth.

FLIGHT

Night in late October. A man walks down Forty-seventh Street, which, at this hour, is nearly deserted. The night is opaque. It blocks out the stars. It clings to him like indeterminate sadness.

Halloween night. Parties are in progress all around the city. In the apartment across the hall from his, for instance. It isn't being alone that he finds disturbing. He prefers it to the eternal compromising that living with someone necessitates. He prefers being able to go for an aimless walk in the middle of the night without having to give anyone an explanation. Paradoxically, it is the aimlessness of this walk that oppresses him.

East Forty-seventh Street, transformed by night, is a brick and mortar ghost town. Tier upon tier of square, lifeless windows wait as if in ambush. The only sounds skittering along these asphalt ravines are uninterpretable echoes. An occasional passing car, a distant pedestrian, and the traffic lights that change from green to amber to red and back to green again are the only vital signs.

Some unusual activity near the Fifth Avenue corner of the street. Several people were collected in front of two large store windows from which the bright yellow light streamed out onto the sidewalk. What was happening? Wasn't that Brentano's? It might be. Or...? Everything looked so different at night.

But wait—it was Brentano's that he visited frequently enough in daytime to leaf through the new books in print and to check how his own titles were selling. A month ago they had had eight copies of his novel *Sandstorm.* The last time he was there, they had had seven. He'd felt a dry gratitude toward the faceless friend who'd bought his book and, in that small anonymous way, validated his efforts.

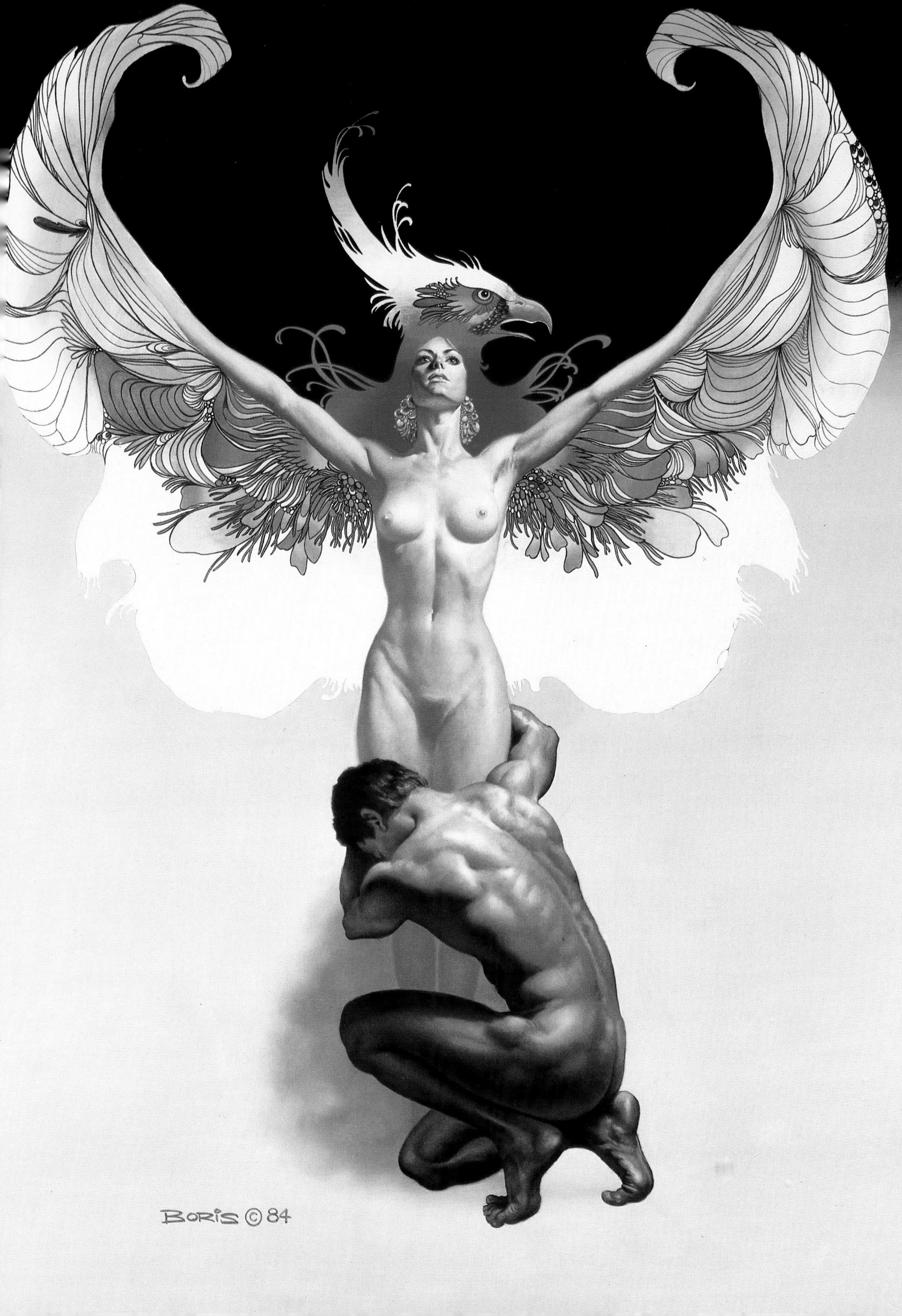
BORIS © 84

Brentano's—with its book-lined walls, its replicas of famous sculptures, its display cases of antique jewelry—which by day was as familiar as his own apartment. It had been transformed into a ballroom.

A costume ball was in progress and the guests were all dressed as characters from fiction. A clever enough publicity idea, he thought. There was Emma Bovary gyrating to a disco beat, her head bobbing rhythmically, her eyes nearly closed. There was Alice in Wonderland bravely following the lead of a bouncing, loose-jointed Sherlock Holmes. Madame Butterfly (a slight-bodied fellow artfully rigged up in black wig, clown white makeup, and flowered kimono) chatting genially with his Lieutenant Pinkerton as they shared a plate of hors d'oeuvres. There was also the Frankenstein Monster who, oblivious to the throbbing rhythms of The Sugarhill Gang, led an audaciously bare-breasted Rima, the bird girl, in a quasi waltz.

Rima...

He pressed against the window, his breath forming a fine mist on the glass.

Rima...

The sheer wild coincidence of seeing her again charged through him like a lightning bolt. Was it actually she? The sight of her full, dark-nippled (had she painted them?) breasts stirred a poignant memory. But it wasn't at all like her to appear at a party in midtown Manhattan half undressed.

Rima, the bird girl. Or was she not Rima but simply a bird? A swan, joined to this lumbering ogre by the artificial intimacy of a dance? A swan, probably. The skirt, richly fluffed out around her hips, was made entirely of white feathers. Her prominent classic nose, her slender neck, her platinum hair swept smoothly back into a bun like a dancer's: so, there she was. He had thought about her, fantasized countless chance meetings with her, formed the clichés of a greeting over and over: *This is a surprise...How have you been...Oh, I've been fine...Getting along...Surviving...*

A small harlequin mask of black silk and rhinestones partially covered her face. Yet there could hardly be any doubt. She cocked her head coyly to one side, said something to the Frankenstein Monster as they danced, and laughed, her carmine lips framing white, even teeth. A phantom wound tugged at him.

She wore a small white cap on her head, and her luxurious, swaying tail feathers reached all the way to the ground. She had to be a swan. Once, when they were still together, she had made an ugly duckling costume—quite unflattering, actually—and worn it (out of some secret resentment, he supposed) to a masquerade party they'd been invited to.

He noted that the Frankenstein Monster was sweating and that the beads of moisture looked like a shiny rash on his scarred forehead. He noted, too, that, as they danced, she caressed the monster's bulky shoulder. Her long purple fingernails might have been talons.

But she could never get her nails to grow that long. They always broke despite all the gelatin capsules she took, despite all the nail-hardening creams she used. *Was this she?* He dismissed the question. He knew her too well. Name, age, favorite foods, pet hates, habits, longings. He knew that she once had wanted to become a professional dancer. Should he have encouraged her more? Would it have made any difference in the long run? At the time it hadn't seemed important. He hadn't taken this dream of hers seriously and, it seemed to him, she hadn't either. She took classes only irregularly. He seldom actually saw her dance—only by coming unexpectedly into a room or (when they lived in a ground floor apartment) by catching sight of her through an open window.

So the duckling had become a swan. Fitting enough, he thought, that she should dress as a bird, having once so abruptly *flown the coop,* as the saying went.

The dance ended. They dropped their arms from around each other and stepped apart. Something glittered in her navel. A rhinestone. It was considerably larger than those in her mask.

"A good thing that I'm around to keep you under control," he had jokingly told her when she confessed a liking for flashy clothes, for sequins and spangles. Since she usually dressed conservatively—sweaters and skirts, sweaters and slacks, in blues, in browns, in grays—he never took that covert flamboyance of hers too seriously either. And now it was rather a surprise, rather jarring in fact, to see the metamorphosis; this exotic creature had no resemblance to his former wife and yet, of course, she did.

The music started again. They moved away, out of his range of vision and into one of the farther rooms.

Brentano's had two doors, through which traffic flowed; the one at which he stood and another one on Fifth Avenue. He hurried around the corner to the other door. He peered in through the glass. People stood around in little groups. She was not among them.

He must find her.

Just inside the door, Marie Antoinette, in a curled wig and false eyelashes, asked to see his invitation. He had neglected to bring it, he said. But he was supposed to meet someone here, an important colleague, an editor. He was a writer, he explained. Why, some of his books were even being sold here at Brentano's.

Marie Antoinette barred his way.

Surely, she could understand. Why, he'd had the invitation in his hand just before he left home and somehow he must have...Through some clumsy oversight...

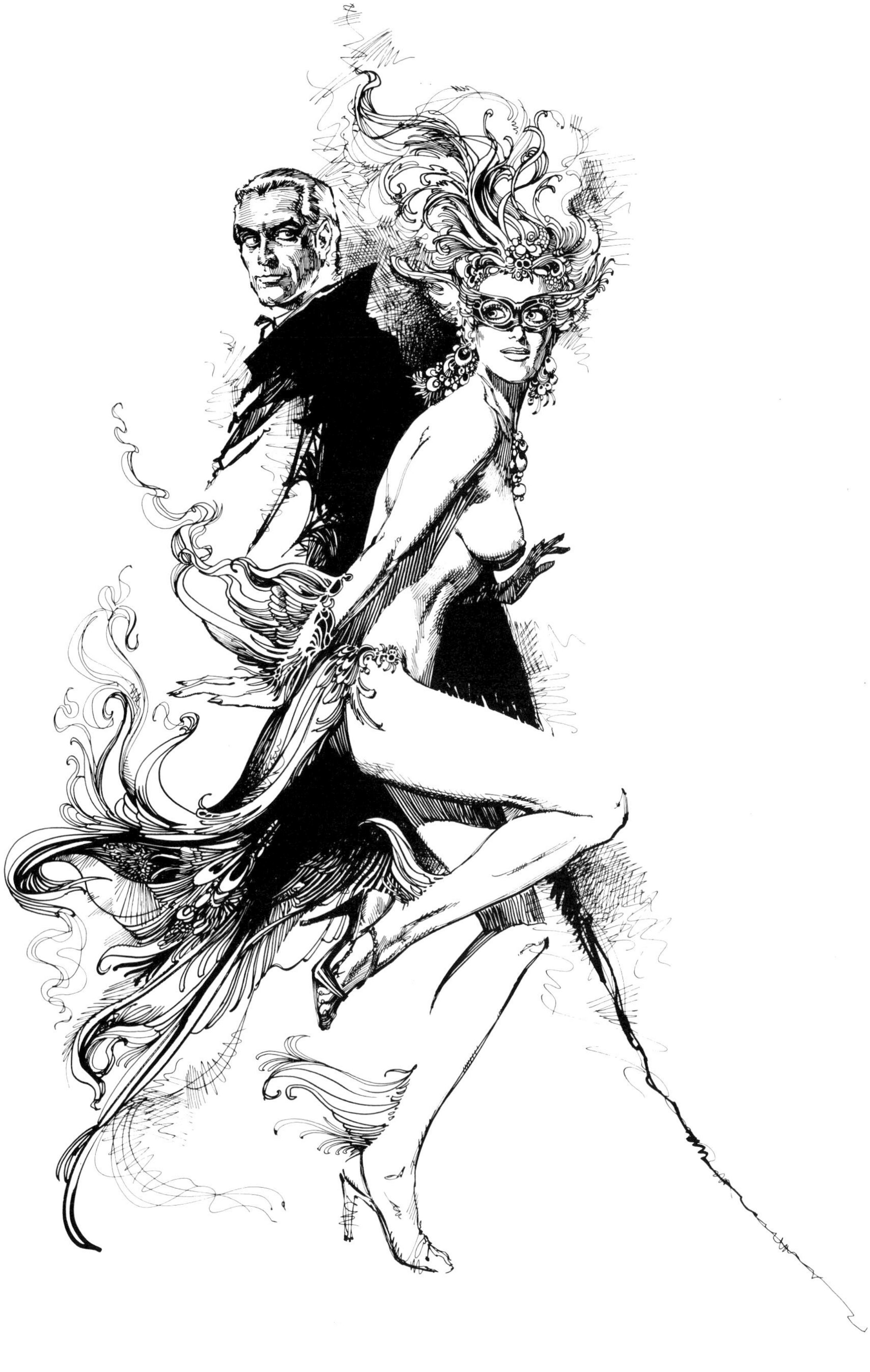

She shook her head. No invitation, no admittance. He went back outside.

Obviously he could not stand guard over both doors at once. He decided to stay near the Fifth Avenue one, through which the main stream of traffic flowed. Twice, however, he rushed around to the other side to see if she might be dancing again. The second time he did see her, though only for a minute or so. She was talking to a man in a royal blue cape, blue plumed hat, and a large papier-mâché sword buckled to his hip. Puss in Boots? The Count of Monte Cristo? Could have been either as far as he was concerned.

Using the Count's shoulder as a ballet barre, she stood on one leg, raised the other, and, skirt drawn up, foot flexed, toe pointed, bent knee nearly touching one magenta-tipped breast, she was—of all things —inviting him to feel her calf muscles.

She had wonderful shapely legs. He'd always told her that. But she preferred not to hear him. Or, in any case, not to listen to any of his comments on her legs—a peculiarity that extended to his touching them.

Sometimes, when they lay in bed together, he liked to run his hand along her body, enjoying the warmth of it and the fine texture of her skin. But she always tensed when he neared her legs, jumped at the slightest contact of finger tips with thighs so that often enough, perversely, he would pounce on her, imprison her under himself, grab here, there, wherever he could, handfuls of buttocks, of belly, of thighs, until she squealed in shrill, giggling hysteria.

"Why don't you like being touched there," he asked her.

"I don't mind it," she answered matter-of-factly.

But she did.

She saw him. Or she looked in his direction and seemed to see him. He thought he could read the question in her masked face: Oh, isn't that...? Yes? No? But before any answer registered she had turned and, with Monte Cristo's silk-sleeved arm about her bare shoulders, disappeared once again into the throng of partners.

"Are you saying that you don't love me anymore?" he had demanded.

"No," she said, pushing her dull, bleached hair back from her peaked face. Her eyes, very round, looked like shiny black marbles. He remembered how strongly, at that instant, she had reminded him of a bird: a pale sparrow unexpectedly confronted with winter, blinking and blinking at the sight of a world grown inexplicably cold and white.

"Is there someone else then?" he had asked.

"No," she said.

No.

But she left him. He had the choice of believing her or not believing her, which, he decided, hardly mattered in the final analysis.

The efforts he made to detain her were feeble rappings on a closed door. Should he have been less phlegmatic? Less concerned about appearing like a beggar in her eyes? Should he have said: Look, I don't want you to go. Can't we talk about it? Can't we find out what's wrong and try to fix it?

On the other hand, she probably would have said: If you don't *know* what's wrong, then there *is* nothing to talk about. Telling her, unequivocally, that he wanted her would have left him too vulnerable to her self-righteous escape. So, he had saved himself. He had pulled through with his self-respect intact.

"I don't understand," he said to her sadly just before her flight to Reno.

She gave him a peculiar searching look. And she gave him a kiss. Not a warm, uncompromising peck on the cheek, but a cruelly arousing one, her tongue slipping enterprisingly into his mouth.

Thus she left him to assuage his longing in whatever way he could.

She left him anew with every woman he made love to, every blond, dark-eyed woman into whose acquiescent body he desperately tunneled hoping to reclaim her.

She left him with every glimpse he caught of her on the street when she turned out, after all, to be someone he did not know.

She left him day after day for months before the thought of her was no longer so acutely painful.

She left Brentano's, finally, on the arm of a tall, satin-caped Dracula. A limousine stood waiting for them at the curb. A gaunt chauffeur in black livery held the door for them as they got in.

He found it ironic that she would choose a vampire —the ultimate thief, the purloiner of human blood —she who condemned the slightest dishonesty, who once, having caught him in a harmless lie, berated him with such furious tears.

He must keep in mind that this was a masquerade and the fellow, sinister as he might look, not an actual vampire. He must disregard the anxiety, the dry mouth, the triphammer pulse in the throat that made it so difficult to articulate his wish to "follow them" to the cabdriver who had fortunately driven up just as the limousine pulled away. But people do reveal their secret personas at masquerades, he thought. They do unmask themselves in the very act of selecting a disguise.

He sat on the edge of the cab's cracked leatherette seat, a pulp-fiction hero hot on the heroine's trail. Suppose she turned around and saw him behind her in the cab, perched on his seat like a squirrel on an ice floe, his salt-and-pepper hair standing on end, his teeth gritted, his jaws clenched with mad determination? In fact, she would never recognize him under the circumstances. But suppose, for the sake of argument, she did. And she asked the chauffeur to stop. And she stepped out of the limo and confronted him, imperiously demanding to know what he was up to? Suppose she was angry? Suppose she said that she had left him because, plainly and simply, she wanted nothing more to do with him?

On the other hand, her leaving was neither plain nor simple if you examined the situation a bit, if you poked beneath the obvious. They *had* meant something to each other. They had, after all, been married for ten years, which was a long time, really, quite a long time for two separate people to be sharing each other's lives. So the relationship had to have been rewarding on some level to have lasted that long. And therefore...

Suppose she gave him a chilly look and said, "I was just treading water for ten years. That was the extent of my reward. I had a good long lesson in how to tread water."

If she did say that, it would only be to hurt him. And if she wanted to hurt him, that in itself would disprove any claim to indifference. When she announced her decision to leave him, it had been without any prelude or warning other than that she spiked her orange juice that morning with a healthy dollop of gin. His initial reaction had been to laugh—out of self-defense, partly. And also because he couldn't think of anything to say.

"Go ahead and laugh,"she said. "The trouble with you is that you have never taken me seriously."

"That's not true," he said. "I do take you seriously when you're serious." He didn't, however. He just could not take the situation (which struck him like something out of a hackneyed soap opera) seriously. Even when she packed her clothes.

"You can't just go," he said to her finally. "You can't."

She turned away from him. "You haven't the slightest idea what I can or can't do."

"Really!" He had affected a supercilious *I know everything there is to know about you* tone. And he had laughed.

There was some truth in her accusation, he thought as he sat in his cab chugging behind her up Park Avenue. He would never have imagined that she could show up at Brentano's with bare breasts and painted nipples. Although she did, come to think of it, have a touch of the exhibitionist in her. One summer she bought a thin cotton dirndle skirt and top through which, when she stood against the light, her nude body was clearly delineated.

"Oh really?" had been her nonchalant answer when he'd drawn this to her attention.

Suppose she did recognize him despite the darkness and the distance between their two cars? Suppose she did tell the chauffeur to let her out and to drive on without her? She'd walk up to his cab, which would stop, she'd look in at him through the window, and say, "So, it is you." He would ask if he could give her a lift. "I might never have recognized you," he would say once she got in, once he saw that recognition had been inevitable. It had been inevitable that he single her out despite her disguise; inevitable that she re-identify him even at night and at a distance; inevitable that they were once again drawn to each other, mouth to mouth, body to greedy, clamorous body.

But she did not see him.

The limousine turned right. He followed.

He followed them to a beige building with a canopied entrance and a doorman. The chauffeur parked in front, remained in the car, and appeared to go to sleep.

He paid his driver and got out of the cab, which went on and turned the corner into Second Avenue. He stationed himself across the street. How long would he have to wait? How much time could the fellow possibly spend in there with his chauffeur sitting outside? Another hour? Two hours? Three?

And then...?

He would ask the doorman to announce him.

And if she had changed her name and the doorman didn't know who he was talking about? Or if she refused to see him? Or if she agreed to see him but when he knocked on the door and she opened it and they stood suddenly face to face she said: "Well, what do you want?"

What did he want, actually?

Nothing.

Nothing at all. Not her surprised, slightly curious recognition. Not her questions about how he was doing. Not a polite, civilized reunion cloyingly tinged with regrets. Not a single platinum hair from her head. Not a single crimson nail paring.

What he wanted (and this he pondered for nearly an hour before he came to the conclusion) was just not to lose her again. What he wanted was to have her, wholly his, lying naked beneath him on cool sheets with her soft arms reaching for him and her legs, spread to embrace him, revealing her downy, beckoning sex.

He already feared her leaving, as if that single act had had more reality than all their years together. What reason was there to hope for a happy reunion? That he wanted it? That he'd been through ten years of exile from her? Ten years of conquests and failures—a pilgrimage from which no one returned unchanged?

He could look her up in the phone book. He could call her tomorrow. Wasn't it idiocy to stand here in the street and wait? The truth of the matter was that a great deal of idiocy existed in the world, most of it difficult to recognize as such until much later. Idiocy as well as wit were subjective, dependent on the point of view of the moment. The most ardently held beliefs could, in retrospect, appear not only fallacious but glaringly aberrant.

"The anguish of others," he once told her, "makes me uncomfortable. I prefer not to be invited along, so to speak, for someone else's botched sky dive."

She accused him of being egocentric.

He accused her of being maudlin.

When she left him, he resolutely concealed his pain. Had he not done so...?

The truth was that there was far too much idiocy in the world that at one time or another paraded as wisdom. At one time wisdom had been letting her go. Now it was winning her back.

Half out on his feet as he was, propped up against the rough brick of the building, his head nodding like a junkie's, he almost missed seeing the fellow leave. It was the limo's motor purring to life that jerked him awake. This was it, then. Count Dracula had taken flight.

This was it.

But he did not move. He waited.

The narrow doorway in which he waited was neutral ground. He was safe there. Beyond it the morning would still come. Beyond it, eventually, he would see her. He might as well wait until he saw her. He had already waited for ten years. A few more hours were inconsequential. All the waiting was simply a preparation for getting her back.

But the waiting reduced him every minute to less than he had been the minute before. He was like a snowman being melted by a pitiless sun. He huddled into himself. He talked to himself from time to time. Violet shadows shifted, deepened, lapped at him like tongues from unseen mouths. He shook himself. Occasionally he jumped up and down to keep warm, to keep awake.

Probably he did doze on and off. The images that passed in front of his eyes had the phantasmal reality of dreams. His sensibilities seemed those of a shadow self.

He has become very small, only an inch or so high. Nevertheless, when she sees him she recognizes him at once and greets him with an unpleasant laugh.

"What's new, little one?" she says. "Writing a world-shaking treatise on termite life?"

He is glad to be so small because that way, regardless of what she says, she can reduce him no further. When she scoops him up and holds him in the palm of her hand, he is not the least bit afraid.

"I could swallow you whole," she says, her lips very close to him, her eyes glistening and alive.

He knows she will not swallow him. He feels quite safe in his defenselessness. Her peculiar morality, he is sure, will prevent her from crushing him, since that would not be much of a victory.

Though she dangles him by one arm just in front of her mouth, all she does is tickle him with her enormous tongue, which is rough and hot against his bare skin. She toys with him, licking his face, his chest, his legs, his tiny sex, which rises in mute salute to her uninhibited ministrations. His very helplessness gives her inordinate pleasure, it seems.

"I'm going to eat you," she whispers teasingly. "I'm going to eat you."

He has grown rigid, paralyzed, waiting for her. Perhaps some rootlike extension of himself now anchors him to the ground. When she appears across the street and he wants to go to her, he cannot move. Nevertheless, she spots him in his no-man's-land and waves to him. He would like to wave back but cannot. His arms are leaden. She comes toward him and he sees, with some surprise, that she is wearing only a sheer diaphanous dress with nothing underneath.

"What's the matter with you, grow roots here?" she says. "Or have you gotten too big, too important for your old friends?"

He says nothing. His tongue, too, is frozen and useless. He hopes, at least, that his eyes will express what he cannot bring himself to say. But no. She is a woman who prefers words to eloquent glances, action to tender, soundless cries of the heart.

"I see you haven't changed a bit," she says. "Still playing the strong silent hero. And still ready as ever, I can see, for a quick little bang." Here she glances at his crotch. His organ bulges like a prizefighter's fist inside his pants. Until this moment he has not been aware of it.

He would like to tell her he loves her, but it is impossible.

"What the hell," she says, apparently not put off by his silence. "For old time's sake."

She raises her filmy skirt up over her shoulders like a cape. For an instant this creates the illusion that she has wings. "For old time's sake," she says, "we'll do it the way you say works for you best." She unzips his pants, turns around, and, standing on tiptoes, slightly bent at the hips, she thrusts herself backward onto his lethally erect penis. Her rounded backside slap-slaps against him with manic force and he remembers how she once commented about the Samurai warriors that they must have tremendous strength to impale themselves on their own swords.

She appears, as expected, just as the sun bleeds its pinks and reds across the sky. She recognizes him but turns away pretending not to. He crosses the street and follows her. She quickens her pace, knowing he is behind her. He continues to close the distance between them and she breaks into a run. He lunges after her. As he is about to catch up to her, she stops short and turns around, causing a collision. He reaches out automatically to keep her from falling and finds himself, jarringly, face to face with her.

At close range he is no longer sure it is she: her pallor, the fluttering pulse in her long, slender throat, her obvious fear.

How is it possible that he never realized what a barbarian he was in her eyes? True, he had failed her. Repeatedly, perhaps. True, he had never admitted that to either of them and, in fact, was not even exactly sure how he had failed. True, the pain he caused her was not more excusable through having been unwittingly inflicted.

But hasn't her leaving evened the account?

Couldn't all their defeats at each other's hands be forgotten? Buried with the past?

"Trust me," he says. But his rasping voice makes the plea sound like a threat.

Trembling violently, she breaks away from him and vanishes, leaving a trail of delicate white feathers settling slowly in her wake. If I follow these, he thinks, picking them up one after the other as he walks, they must lead me to her again.

He awoke, fully at least, when the morning was already well along. A steel claw of anxiety fastened on him. She had emerged from the canopied doorway across the street and was walking down the half-moon driveway. She wore an angora coat—white as the feathers he had gathered in his dream—and her silvery hair was piled high as a crown on her head.

He stepped from his doorway and hurried after her. He stumbled over the curb, his legs not quite under control. At least he didn't fall. His body ached from having remained still so long. At the end of the block he caught up to her.

She did not recognize him at first, possibly because she did not expect to see him. But her uncertain expression put him precariously on the edge of panic. Luckily, she smiled, and he was able to breathe.

"How have you been?" she asked.

He suggested that they stop in somewhere for an early lunch if she had no other particularly pressing appointment.

"Are you seeing anyone?" she asked, taking a sip of dry white wine. He thought she asked out of politeness rather than real curiosity. He would have liked to be able to tell her: Yes. Oh yes, I'm seeing a fascinating woman who . . . But he contented himself with merely shaking his head.

A seascape hung behind her on the wood-paneled wall. Plants hung from the ceiling: Swedish ivy, wandering jew. He wondered how they grew so abundant in artificial light.

"I have often wondered how you were doing," she said.

"I saw you in Brentano's last night," he confessed after her salad and his minute steak arrived.

"And you followed me?" She did not sound particularly surprised.

"It was odd seeing you after all this time. Especially disguised as a swan."

"It wasn't much of a disguise," she said with a curtness that made him reply quickly,

"I only meant that if I'd had to venture a guess as to what character from fiction you would dress up as I might sooner have said, knowing you, that you'd choose to be the Little Mermaid from Anderson's fairy tales or, maybe, the Girl with the Red Shoes."

"You don't know me," she said.

He might have defended himself. Instead he asked if she didn't think past mistakes could be forgotten.

"Past mistakes," she said solemnly, "can easily trigger uncontrollable laughter."

He remembered how, indeed, she could be gripped by such spells of unaccountable laughter she would end in tears. And how, once, when she'd seemed quite unable to stop crying, he had held her close for a long time without saying anything at all.

It could be that she also remembered this. Her whole mood abruptly changed, lightened, became flirtatious. She asked if he wanted to accompany her to Central Park where she was going to see the ducks and the wild geese that still remained. And the swans.

Were there swans in Central Park? At this time of the year?

Definitely, she assured him.

She saw them before he did: patches of light interwoven with the weeping willow's low-hanging branches. They might have been no more than that. Patches of light shimmering on the water.

"There they are," she said.

Miraculously, two splendid swans detached themselves from the light and the willow branches and glided toward them across the silken lake.

Her affinity for those regal birds was fascinating to watch. Still, a kind of jealousy stabbed at him. She knelt on the bank and threw pebbles into the water. They fell just short of the birds, which, apparently, were not afraid. They thrust their heads under the water, retrieved the pebbles, and brought them back to her, laying them in her upturned palms. It was a game from which he was excluded. A totally pointless game.

After a while, though, she leaped up and sprinted off, initiating a different game, in which he must try to catch her.

He ran. Breathless. Lungs bursting.

How quickly she reached the far cluster of trees. He must not let her disappear. Must not lose her again. He hurled himself up the grassy slope and caught her just as she would have vanished into the thicket. She stopped, unexpectedly, so that he ran headlong into her. He caught her, his arms going tight around her, pulling her on top of him as they fell gently and very slowly to the ground.

"I won't ever let you go again," he said as she began to kiss him—hungry little kisses, like bites, on his lips, his cheeks, his eyelids. Her kisses, so passionate, stung his eyes, blurred his vision.

Her hands, like beating wings at his clothes... *I love you... love you... always loved you...*

The heat of her body. The rising and falling dance. The grinding dance of locking interlocking thighs. The ground is hard against his back. But she is soft, pliant, opening to his touch.

He is panting, breathless, his lungs bursting, his blood—dammed up against his eardrums—pounding. He wants to transfix her, possess her, fuse with her so

she cannot ever leave him again.

"I'll never let you go," he cries, searching the surface of her for entrances, squeezing, kneading, filling his hands with the wonder of her.

Her mouth, her tongue, her pearl-white teeth. Her kisses sting his eyes, blur his vision, and he sees her as if in a dream: a beautiful white cloud descending on him from the sky. The dream transforms him. He is flying, flying enveloped in clouds, immersed in clouds, wrapped and rewrapped and thrust free of them, in and out. Flying...

When he came down to earth the sky was clear and cold. He sat up and looked about. He did not see her. The tall, dry grass obstructed his view. He called her. She did not answer.

It was the end of autumn and he sat, half undressed, among the dead weeds and bushes in Central Park. How had it happened that he lost her? She had been so real when he held her in his arms, real as her absence was now. He pulled on his clothes, shivering inside them.

The waist-high dead weeds, broken where they had lain together, seemed to have been fashioned into a kind of nest around him.

He comes down to earth.

The sky is cold and blue. The broken weeds and dry grasses in which he lies have been woven into a sort of nest. As he shiveringly pulls on his clothes, he discovers a beautiful golden egg beside him in the nest. It is as large as a human heart.

WOLVES

She had auburn hair, hazel eyes, and pale, nearly white skin that freckled readily in direct sunlight. She was 5'5", slender, and often taken for a dancer although her gracefulness was natural and she remained largely unaware of it. She was quiet and usually kept to herself. Though she wished she could be closer to others, she made no attempt to be. Instead, she watched them from a distance, believing that, in any case, she could read their gestures, their facial expressions, their thoughts, and therefore they would have nothing more to tell her. Their concerns, on the whole, struck her as frivolous; their values, superficial. What she longed for were real friends, not make-believe ones.

Sometimes she deliberately provoked these others—not that she was immune to their opinions of her, but rather because she enjoyed baiting those from whose circle she had been excluded. Clearly, though, this cat-and-mouse game worked as a further barrier between herself and others.

She rationalized her situation: companionship was simply a ruse to conceal isolation, ebullient chatter simply a mask to conceal despair, stylish clothes a camouflage for flaccid bodies, solicitous overtures a disguise for selfish intents. Appearances could well be peeled away one after the other like the skins of an onion. The trick was to stop at the last tightly curled inner skin before the *no-thing-ness* at the core of it all was revealed.

Already, years before, when those she secretly longed for called her names or ran from her, she decided that behind their human faces they had to be primitive and inhuman. Since, as evolving embryos, they passed through fish and reptile stages, some intrinsic part of their souls must have been arrested along that way. She had no doubt that many of them were bats and hyenas behind their assumed humanism. And that there were plenty of frogs parading as princes. She hoped there was such a thing as a real prince.

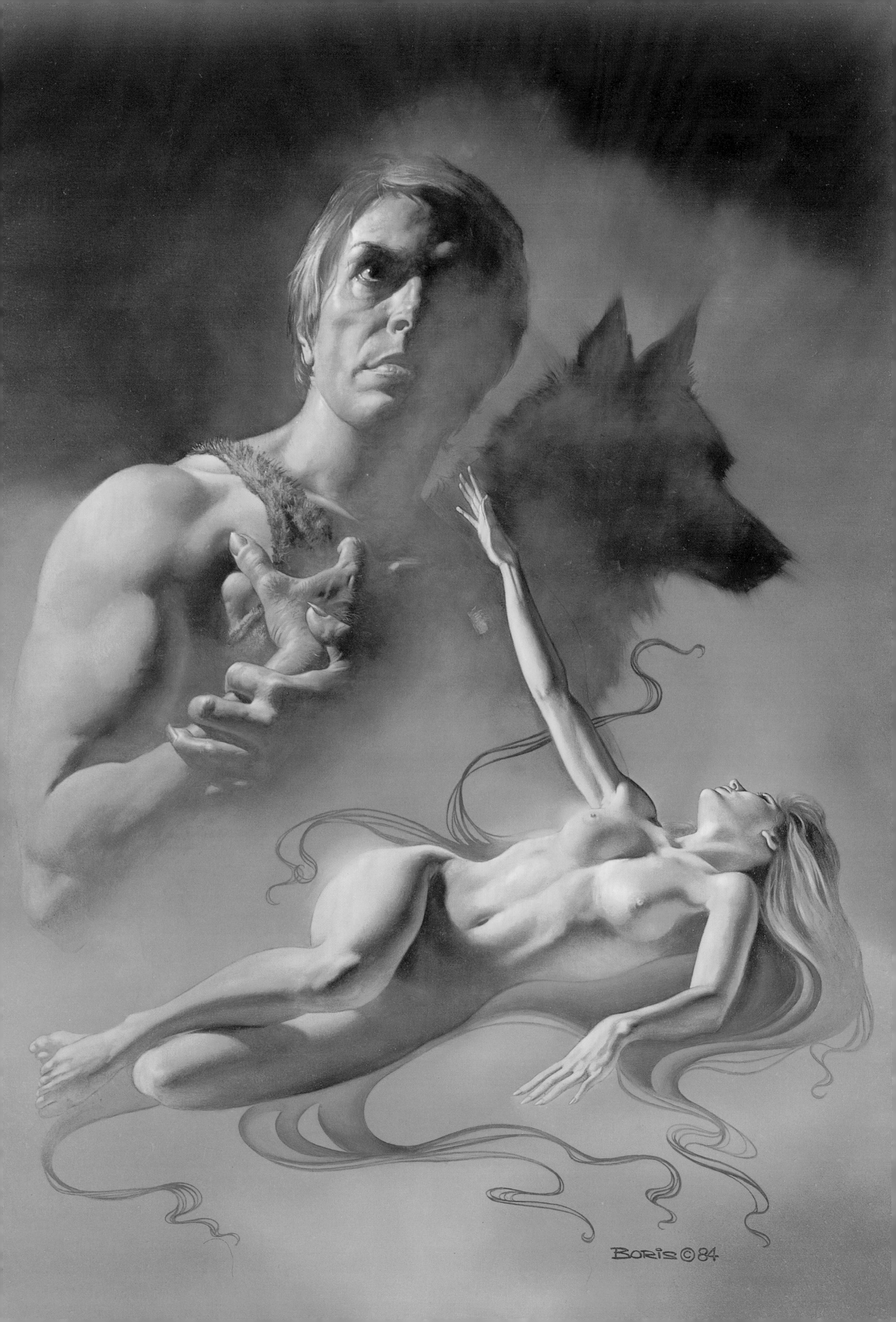
BORIS © 84

Occasionally she took a lover for a night or a week. These lovers invariably turned out to be toads, chameleons, weasels behind their human posturings. She invariably awoke in their arms to judge them and to judge their remembered grunts and yelpings and mewlings. Thus it always became clear to her between the beginning and the end that she had, again, chosen the wrong one.

The rumors about the so-called wolf-man intrigued her. As well as his intimidating aura that kept everyone at a distance. She did not find his thick, long hair offensive. Or his clothes: the shaggy fur vest worn over his bare chest, the heavy leather boots, the faded blue jeans that gloved a provocative bulge of cock and a firm ass. His sensuality, his muscular torso, his eyes in which a savage intensity glittered, his mouth curved into the slight suggestion of an ironic smile—it seemed altogether credible that a wolf hunkered inside this casing. How the rumors evolved was obvious. It was to his credit, she thought, that he made no attempt to deny them.

Was it or was it not a mistake to pursue this man? Nothing had actually been proven against him. There was not a single eyewitness to attest to his shape shifting.

A man is supposed to be a man, they said. *A wolf is supposed to be a wolf.* And based on these simplistic distinctions, they damned him. Because his joys and griefs differed from theirs, because his dreams stunned them, his hungers repelled them, they condemned him.

Why couldn't they leave him to his strangeness, his despairs, his destined longings, and his pleasures? A wolf-man had a soul, after all.

She first saw him at the Quarter Moon Bar which, to judge from its rustic decor, had once been a stable. It was frequented by students, aspiring writers, artists, and the usual sprinkling of dedicated drinkers. She herself had consumed glass after glass of wine that evening, counting on it to dispel a formless angst that haunted her.

A light rain had fallen. The wet sidewalks under the streetlights glistened like ice while in the bar the air congealed with cigarette smoke and the heat of bodies. Really now, she thought, I am just wasting my time. I should get out of here. She did not live far from the Quarter Moon and might even have found the walk refreshing. However, she made no effort to go.

Any moment..., she said to herself. *Any moment now...* She felt as if she were sitting on the lid of some Pandora's box against which a host of shadowy bats beat their hollow-boned wings. At any moment the lid could fly up letting the things escape to shrill their high nightmare cries at a stupefied world. Fortunately there was an element of choice: she could let them go or she could keep them locked up.

It was precisely as she was thinking these thoughts that he entered the bar. Those who had automatically turned toward the door looked quickly away at their companions or their drinks. No one moved from their places and yet there was a subtle shift in the room, as if the air now flowed in a different direction. As if a space had been cleared for him. Their glances momentarily locked and she felt his brief appraisal, like a whip crack, stinging clear to the bone marrow. Then the door swung closed behind him. A wisp of cooler air that she may only have imagined was lost. He scanned the smoky room for a place to sit.

Any moment..., she had thought. And there he was. It was inevitable, of course.

The previous week she had been sitting in a booth at the back. Walking, her usual antidote for restlessness, had not helped. And so she ended up at the Quarter Moon drinking wine way past midnight and thinking there must be a way to shut out the ceaseless plaguing premonitions, some way to sleep without awakening in a cold sweat.

An old woman came into the bar. She knew her slightly: a pariah; dull, tangled hair wound into a nest on her head, tentish threadbare coat anchored around her waist with a rope. She'd seen her begging on the street from time to time and had once given her two dollars. It was unlikely that the woman would remember her, yet she felt suddenly uncomfortable. The woman shuffled slowly on arthritic limbs, stopping at each occupied table and booth to say something that was met with little interest. She moved with the stolid seeming strength of those whose stiffened limbs no longer bend. At last she came to the end booth where the young woman sat.

"Your fortune?" she asked. "Would you like to have your fortune told?" Shadows held permanent sway in her ruined face.

"Yes. Why not." She had intended not to answer at all, merely to shake her head. But there was no actual harm in it, was there. At worst it would be an interesting distraction.

The old woman sat down opposite her and unwound a wrinkled silk scarf from around a deck of cards. The scarf smelled of dry rose petals. What sort of fortune would she tell, this desiccated crone?

"What is it that troubles you?"

Let her find out. Let her tell me, the young woman thought even as it was on the tip of her tongue to say: I don't understand why my feelings seem so alien, not

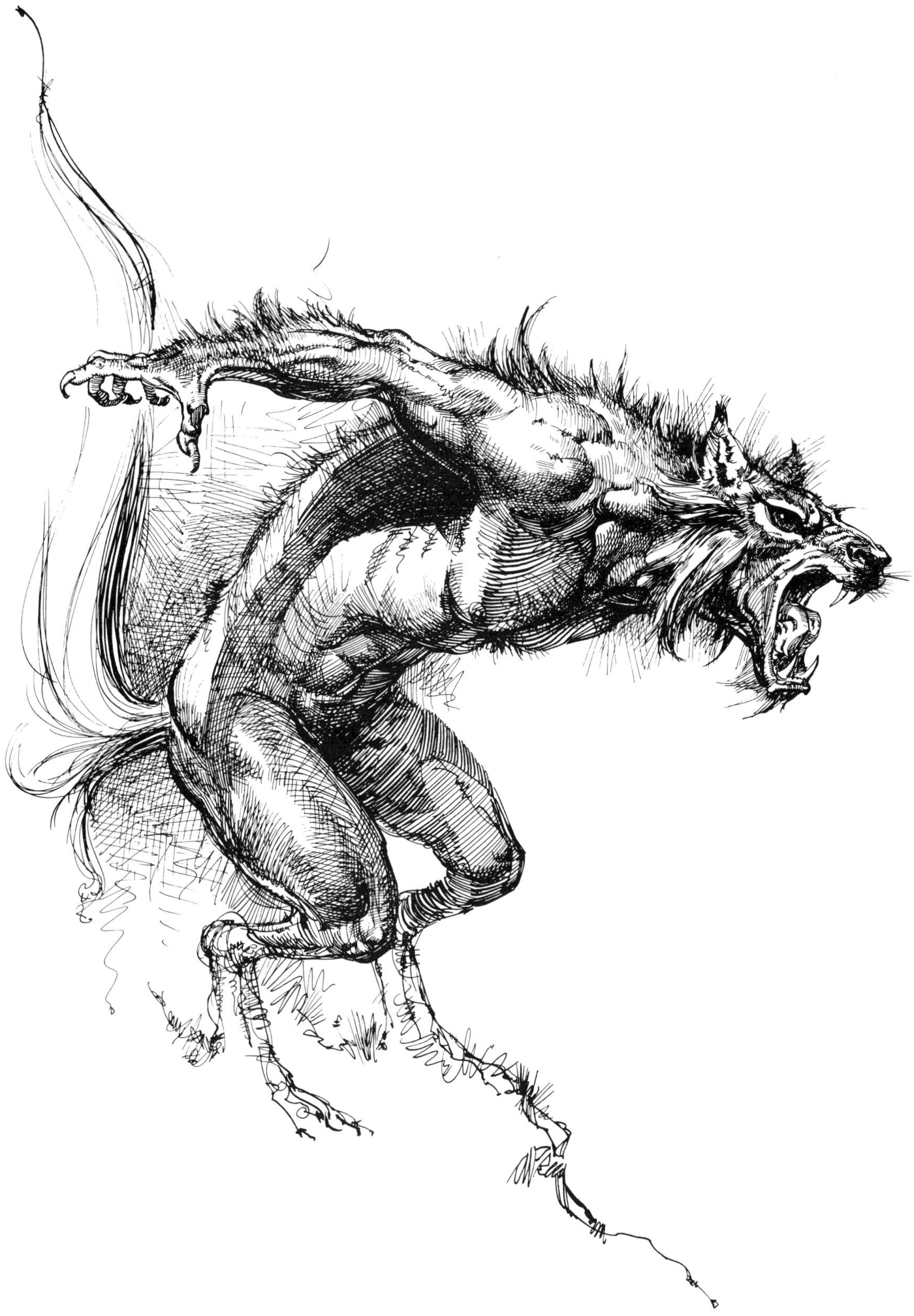

mine at all but like those of a stranger. "I don't know," she said instead. "Something I can't define."

The old woman shuffled the cards, asked her to cut them, laid them out on the table in the pattern of a cross, and studied them for some minutes.

"You have no close ties." She spoke in a singsong voice without expression. "Your father disappeared before you were born and you avoid thinking of your mother. But, because you resemble her so strongly, it happens..."

An unexpected sadness invaded her heart. But the old woman was talking about the past and it was the future she should be reading. The future as it lay in front of her on the table; the colored medieval pictures waiting to be interpreted: the skeleton knight in black armor, the two gray dogs howling at the half moon, the bat-winged satyr perched on a pillar to which a naked man and woman stood chained.

The old woman bent closer to the cards. Was the future visible to her? And if it was, why did she start with the past? Likely enough she was a fake, a wretched, decaying creature just trying to scratch up a few dollars. But she had touched a delicate memory. One outgrew one's past only tangentially, the young woman knew. The past did intrude on the future; did leave its mark, its wounds; did have the power to paralyze at times.

"The card of death," the old woman said. "In this case it indicates a journey; not a journey in the usual sense, however." She paused for a moment and then continued. "Not a physical move from one place to another. Here, you see, in combination with these other cards it suggests what you might call an internal journey; a growing and changing of the spirit, so to speak. The card of death..."

Her mother sat in a chair by the window making dolls for her out of old stockings; a Red Ridinghood doll and a wolf doll. She began by mending all the holes in the stockings. Was this to keep death out? For years it did work. For years she believed in the magic circle of her mother's warmth where there was no death. People did die somewhere in the world. But these corpses chanted their dirges of loss too far away to matter.

"I would like to fall in love," the young woman said.

The fortune-teller collected the cards, reshuffled them, asked her to cut them, and laid them out.

"I see that you are isolated from others. I can tell you that in some sense this will change. As you see, here again is the card of death, indicating a spiritual journey. You are going to fall in love. That is perfectly clear. But the man you love will, at the same time, curiously repel you."

The young woman shifted in her seat.

"You want to see him?" the fortune-teller asked, and pushed a card toward her. "Here he is."

The King of Swords. Regal, solemn; seated on a massive throne, he held a sword like a gleaming scepter in his hand.

"You will meet him quite soon. Within the week, I should say."

"Yes," the young woman murmured. The King of Swords. The little picture on the card seemed to gain dimension as she studied it. The King: his muscled body, his mute ferocity, his strangely menacing attraction. He was darkness, mysterious and sinister. And he was light gleaming like a distant jewel in the portentous night.

I won't do anything, she thought. I won't even look at him. Yet, when he left she was suddenly so agitated that she too got up, put some money on the table to pay for her wine, and left. When she emerged from the Quarter Moon, he was nowhere in sight. She ran to the nearest corner, which opened onto Sheridan Square.

He might have gone in any direction. Or he might have taken the subway. The subway entrance, its stairs going darkly down into the earth, offered no clue. Was she relieved? She had, in truth, no good reason for following him. She didn't actually know him. Nor did the fortune-teller's prediction give her any special right. Yet to lose him so easily was a disappointment. She had expected... She was not sure what she had expected. The next time I see him..., she thought.

The next time occurred soon enough.

She had gone to the Quarter Moon around midnight for three nights running. She had asked about him and was told what she already knew: that he was a good man to steer clear of.

Her quest was bizarre. She readily admitted it to herself. The admission did nothing to alter her behavior or banish the pictures that paraded ceaselessly through her mind:

A silver crescent moon eerily lights a meadow in which a couple makes love. Unaccountable flashes of light play across their features from time to time. A woman in the lust-maddened embrace of a man she does not know and who is, to all appearances, not entirely human. The pervasive sense of manic joy and imminent danger; the suggestion of hell as divine delight.

On the third night of her vigil, he appeared. She was sitting at the bar. The place was crowded. A jungle chatter of voices mingled with the dissonant blat of a pop tune that swelled from the jukebox. She felt rather than saw him enter. She did not dare turn around. Instead she watched him in the back bar mirror. He seemed to be looking for someone (for her?) whom he did not see. When he left, she gave him no more than a minute's head start and then followed.

This time she saw him turn from Christopher Street onto Seventh Avenue. She followed him from there onto Fourth Street, then onto Hudson, then onto Little West Twelfth, after which he kept on straight toward the river. Here, among the locked meat-packing factories and warehouses, among the endless gray planes of silent buildings and loading platforms and empty pavements, he disappeared.

A cat, pursued by the silence, dashed across the street and also disappeared. She was struck by the feeling that she too might have vanished into this landscape that absorbed all color and sound, save that her blood was crashing too loudly through her veins, her heart ticking off each instant too precisely. Her eyes traveled the brick walls like a blind man's hand in search of doors.

A man's silhouette had been spray-painted on the corner of a building: half crouching, his powerful flanks bare, his muscles quivering with tension, his hands gnarled, his pointed ears alert, his snout wide open in a soundless howl; the painted shape might or might not have moved just before she saw it.

A painted shape or a shadow?

Paint. It had to be. There was nothing nearby to cast such a shadow. Yet she knew appearances could be inconclusive. The windowless architecture, the uncanny silence, the huge trash barrels lowering at the far end of a loading platform like actors awaiting some terrible cue ... They might all cloak some profounder reality.

There was another silhouette painted on the brick of a farther wall. And another beyond that. And several on the building across the street. She could run. She could still run. There was still time to get away before those shapes, ferocious and inhuman, detached themselves from the wall, closed in on her, cut off her escape. But she stood motionless, helpless, the impulse to run exploding in her brain, never reaching her feet.

The nightmare shifted; the shadows became opaque.

He stepped suddenly in front of her from a doorway that had not existed before. His eyes gleamed gold beneath the street lamp's cream-gray haze.

"What do you want?" His breath on her face was sweet as blood.

"To know you." A guileless answer. All others escaped her.

He grasped her hair and jerked her head back so that the lamp light fell full on her face. "Don't," he said. "You may not like what you get once you have it."

She wanted to tell him to let go of her hair. She drank his sanguinary breath. Her forced her toward the doorway from which he'd emerged; thrust her into the shadows that were stone hard against her back. He pressed himself against her. He crushed the air from her lungs. His tongue was a truncheon in her mouth: gouging, bruising.

And, abruptly, he released her.

"Get out of here," he snarled. "Get the hell out of here."

The fleeing *tap-tap* of her shoes against the pavement filled the street with footsteps, running, the sounds of a chase; the sounds of a pack of shadows chasing her: panting, growls, scorching breath on the back of her neck, the air thick with the delirium of those phantom hunters. She ran as fast as she could and did not look back.

The aching to see him again began as soon as she felt safe. The absent lover is doubly loved. And in his absence she re-created him. She shaped him. She had little difficulty adapting him to her dreams. She drew his portrait from memory with a charcoal pencil so she could keep him with her. So she could look at him whenever she wanted to. And still he remained elusive. He watched her out of enigmatic eyes. He charmed her and scorned her, rejected her and bound her to himself. She did not struggle against loving him.

But the love that might have remained no more than a dream became a fiery wailing in her heart, out of which he was born and reborn for her, out of which he knelt over her dreaming lips and breasts and thighs, his strong body obliterating the horizon. Out of which he locked her wrists together with one huge paw, and his claws and his cock went exploring. Out of which she twisted under him, spread-legged and moaning as his kisses slammed through her blind flesh evoking vision upon vision. Out of which he carved an opening into her that glistened like moonlight, starlight, wonder.

A dead man was found near Little West Twelfth Street, his pockets turned inside out, the apparent victim of a robbery. Except (and this gave rise to further agitated talk about werewolves) that he had been neatly eviscerated. The awful wound across his abdomen was said to have looked like a grinning mouth. She heard about it and shrugged her shoulders as if to say: In a large city all sorts of things happen.

It wasn't that she discounted the threat of werewolves. Or even that she felt particularly safe from their frightening hungers. But danger existed on a wholly separate level from passion. That hers was a passion, a need she hardly understood, made it difficult to speak of. And to whom should she have spoken of it in any case?

She slept a great deal. Sleep used to offer a reliable escape from burdens that always seemed lighter in the morning. She had come to rely on a measure of absolution to appear with the sunrise. But these days, shadows appeared with the sun. And all day long they lengthened.

What am I doing? she wondered. This distracting, obsessive passion seemed to arise out of familiar things: the hollow of a pillow where her head had lain, which would remind her that she was alone; the warmth caught between the bed sheets, which, again, was just hers. A long dead flower, still inexplicably sweet, discovered between the pages of a book.

Quite likely, its true origin was less benign. Quite likely it began with a mutant cell that grew painlessly in the soul. At first one experienced only a slight alteration of the blood flow, an unaccustomed breathlessness at the mildest exertion. That startled awareness of the malignant lump (like a newer, stronger second heart pumping ruthlessly away) always came too late. By that time the very thought of excising it only fueled its growth. It palpitated visibly under the breast. It directed one's thoughts, one's dreams, one's actions. By the time one became aware of it one was like an arrow launched from a bow, cruising with apparent effortlessness toward the fated target.

Eleven P.M. The street noises had faded. The street itself had faded, as had the room in which she waited for him. Only his portrait stood out clear and strong. She could read his resolve in the charcoal eyes she had drawn. He gazed out of the paper at her with the single-minded intensity of an animal assessing the movement of shadows.

He could come to her now. There would be nothing to stop him. He would not even have to knock on the door, which was unlatched. He could come in without a word. He could lie down beside her on the narrow bed. He could turn to her, press his body against hers, tell her a love story without words, his kisses on her listening flesh spinning the magic tale.

But he would not come here. Yes, they kept watch over each other. Still, she must make the initial moves. She must get up, wash, perfume herself, paint the face of a seductress (blue eyelids, hectic pink cheeks, a carmine mouth) over her paler one, put on black satin pants and slip a sheer white blouse over her naked breasts.

Was it or was it not a mistake to pursue this man? What the others saw was a brute who offended their sensibilities, a madman, a renegade, someone whose simple presence was a threat. What she saw was a man who was not at war with himself, who had exploited his strengths and accepted his limitations, a giant who feared neither the savagery nor the gentleness of his nature.

Was this view absurdly romanticized? Was it safer to follow the authoritative flow of popular opinion? All her life she had been unsure of her decisions. Foresight was a thing of chance. But she knew why the gods offered so little direction. It was more entertaining to watch their creatures argue with echoes and dance with apparitions.

It was crowded at the Quarter Moon when she arrived. He was already there. She had the impression that he was waiting for her. Certainly he knew she was coming. She pretended not to recognize him and made her way through the laughter and noise directly to the bar. She ordered a glass of wine. When it was put in front of her, she grasped the stem of the glass and stared into the amber liquid to avoid the temptation of watching him. Yet from time to time her eyes strayed on their own and she found herself gazing at his dark, glowering face. He stared at her without pretense. Brazenly. His thoughts beat in her brain like eagle wings: *I'm warning you . . . warning you . . .*

The surrounding crowd blurred as he came into sharper focus, each coarse, curling hair on his head, each tiny line, each pore. His eyes, unnaturally yellow and bright, reflected the light of some feverish moon. His large hands, motionless, resting on his thighs, were stained with something darkish. Blood, she imagined. And the fur on the front of his vest was matted with it.

Did she emit the odor of excitement? Of fear? He rubbed his hands slowly, deliberately, against the tight fabric of his pants. To clean off the blood? Because he, too, had become aware of it? No, he would hardly be so fastidious. Rather, it was a signal. He reached into his pocket, brought forth a bill, and laid it on the table. She snapped suddenly awake. He was already at the door when she jumped off the bar stool to follow him.

Luckily she had followed him once before or she would again have been at a loss. A group of people left the Quarter Moon as he did and their shuffling, chattering exit delayed her just long enough. When she got to the street, he was gone.

Seventh Avenue was bright with tourists, vagrants, Saturday night strollers, and the continuous flare of headlights streaming south. West Fourth Street, narrower, was markedly emptier. The street lamps threw a pale haze that only served to emphasize the surrounding darkness.

Hudson Street.

How curiously the invading darkness altered the landscape. Hudson Street, with its small stores and six-story apartment houses, seemed to have metamorphosed into a flat swath of gray earth from which the buildings on either side rose starkly as mountains into the sky. Was the night in league with him? A slight breeze carried the ghostly chirrup of a tree frog on its ripples.

Little West Twelfth Street, also mysteriously changed, was a cul-de-sac. Its windowless buildings, dense as a forest, shut it off from the rest of the world. She could go no farther. The path ended and she stopped, uncertain. She looked around for the painted wolf-men, half afraid to see them, their fiery eyes like live coals in that eerie tapestry of grays and blacks. But there was no sign of them. A queer, creeping excitement spread through her. She sensed his nearness as strongly as if he stood just behind her, as if his hands were just about to close on her neck.

A full moon rose, pale and stark. It carved shadows out of this wilderness. Dozens of them. The longer she stood there, the more she could see. Night vision did not stop at the surface of things but enveloped them, penetrated them. She saw the shadows gather, take on new contours, solidify. She saw their hearts quicken, their mute rapture float toward her on swells of air. She stood, transfixed, breathing them in.

The howl, clear, resonant, awesome as thunder, filled the space between sky and earth; a disquietingly seductive ballad. Its vibrations rose up from the ground

through her feet and along her spine. It kindled a strange exhilaration. It caused the hair on her neck to rise. The shadows she watched rustled and brushed together. Something was moving among them.

There exists within the soul a creature to which one may, all one's life, remain deaf and blind. Like the occupant of a room next to one's own of whom one is ignorant. One may be awakened one night by the anonymous neighbor's stirring and moaning. One may go back to sleep. Or, one may press an ear against the wall and feel it throb, feel it panting.

That is how it happens. As easily as that. One awakens. The wall has become membrane thin. Something is moving behind it. The wall rips. A face appears through the rip. It is the face one has known and not known all along: the face of the monster run from in dreams; the face of the ideal lover; the face fleetingly glimpsed now and then behind the familiar one reflected in mirrors. Terrifying and beautiful, it is the reverse side of that known face: the inner face.

The notes of the wolfsong are invisible hands that, stroking, remold her. She does not begin and end where she used to, in scalp, in fingertips, in toes. She unfolds as gently as a blossom to the sun. The distance from her eyes to the ground grows shorter. The perfume of wild things intensifies, as does the rich, captivating musk that she identifies as his.

The thing that was moving among the shadows separates from them. For a moment only she hesitates. And then she eagerly trots toward it on clawed, padded feet.

EXORCISM

The setting resembles a psychiatrist's office: desk, swivel chair behind the desk, armchair in front of it, leather couch, end table replete with Kleenex, framed medical degrees on the wall, an air conditioner emitting a steady white-sound hum. All the props give the impression of having been hurriedly accumulated; the whole scene might be dismantled in moments to reveal a backstage of beams, lights strung on poles, painted flats propped against one another. For instance, one might see the flat on which a garden has been painted leaning against another flat depicting the gaudy interior of a nightclub behind which, in turn, the graying wall of a prison cell would be partly revealed. The scene is clearly meant to be that of a psychiatrist's office, yet it evokes the sense of a false reality, a facade against which players will be presented in a chaotic sequence.

You could say I'm here because I'm afraid.
I could say that, perhaps. But I'm more interested in what you have to say.
What I have to say? (Pause.) Well, I have to say I'm here because they are afraid.
I see. And what are they afraid of?
Me.
They're afraid of you?
Yes.
But you're not afraid.
Sure I am. I've always been afraid. But as far as coming here goes, that was their idea.
And what are you afraid of? Can you tell me?
Everything. (Pause.) Nothing.
Can you be more specific than that?
I can.
Please.

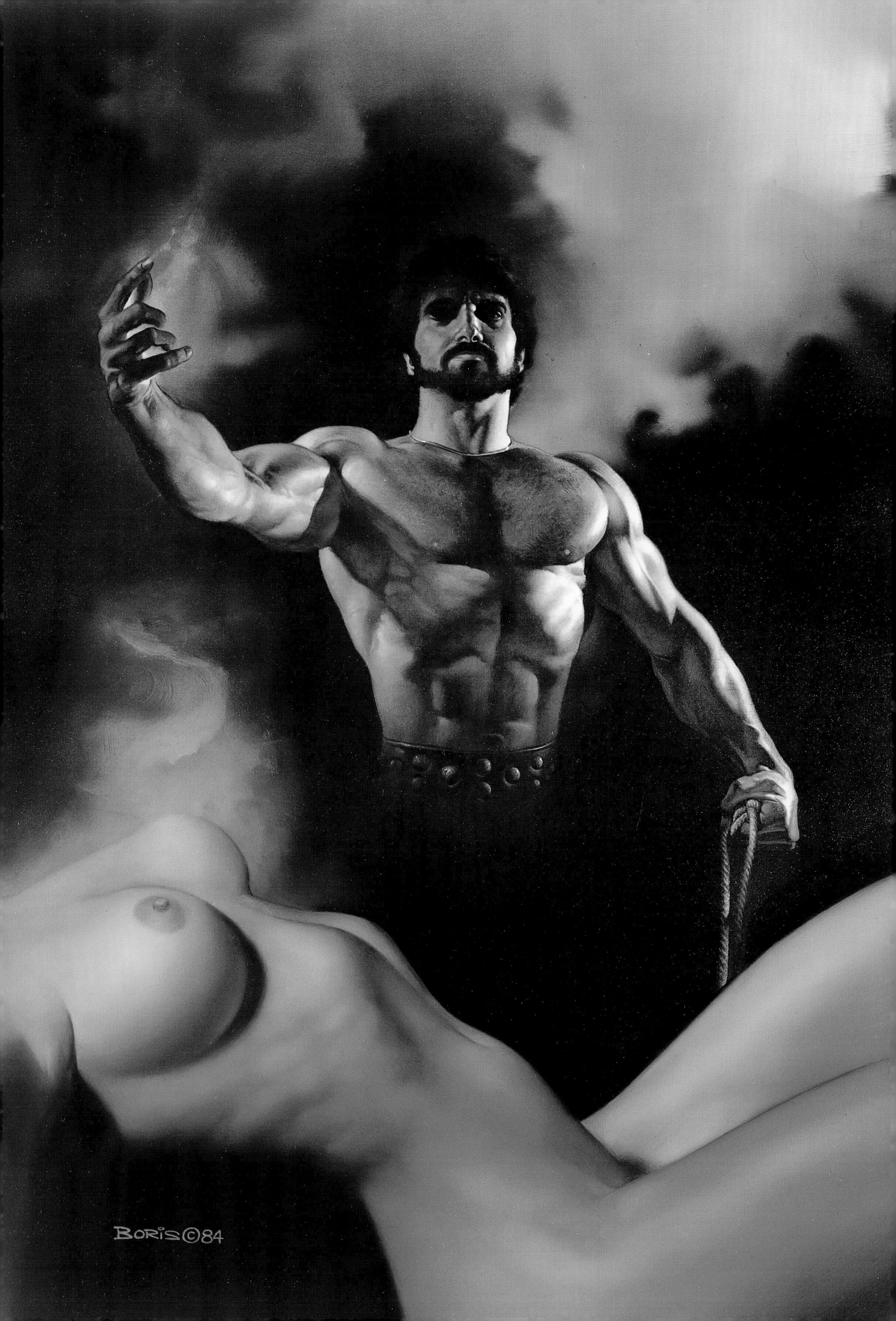
BORIS©84

(Another pause. She smiles flirtatiously. His face remains impassive. Her smile slowly fades.)

If I were a juggler I would be afraid of dropping one of the balls.

But you're not a juggler.

If I were a sheep I would be afraid of goats.

But you are not a sheep.

If I were a shadow I would be afraid of the night.

But you are not a shadow.

I don't find it particularly helpful for you to tell me what I am not.

Why don't you tell me what you are.

I am afraid.

Of what?

(Her smile reappears, much bolder, more obviously seductive.)

Of the body and the spirit engaging each other in cannibal rites.

He finds her answers evasive. He doesn't consider that this may be due to the banality of his questions. He believes fears are what distinguish one human being from another. He discounts the idea that individuality may be shaped by trivia, like one's name, for example. And the role one might, sheerly by default, have chosen to play in the world. I can still hear his voice, colorless as windowglass, so clearly tracking her answers to seeming dead ends.

How would you define the word *love*? What is it for you?

Spiritual love, you mean? Or are you talking about physical love?

Either. Both, if you have different definitions of them.

Of course they're different.

And...?

Spiritual love is a nightmare in the heart. Physical love is simply a growling in the cunt.

She distrusted him, she explained one afternoon, mainly because of the nature of his work: he invariably dealt with losers for which she, personally, felt a healthy aversion if not outright contempt. And in someone who obviously considered her a loser, she could not have any faith.

Why are you here?

The family first noticed her peculiarly changed attitude toward the cat. They had been so accustomed to the sight of her with the churlish creature curled up 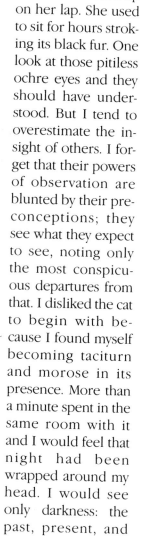 on her lap. She used to sit for hours stroking its black fur. One look at those pitiless ochre eyes and they should have understood. But I tend to overestimate the insight of others. I forget that their powers of observation are blunted by their preconceptions; they see what they expect to see, noting only the most conspicuous departures from that. I disliked the cat to begin with because I found myself becoming taciturn and morose in its presence. More than a minute spent in the same room with it and I would feel that night had been wrapped around my head. I would see only darkness: the past, present, and future only in gradations of black.

I would like to talk about why you felt like killing your cat.

Because I hated it.

You didn't always hate it.

It didn't always hate me, either.

And you're sure that it does now?

Of course. And, to anticipate your next question: I don't feel that my reaction is at all extreme. Who hasn't ever hated enough to feel like killing? We're all murderers in our secret hearts.

Would you consider it possible that you are attributing thoughts and feelings to the cat which, in fact, it doesn't have?

It's always watching me.

And you don't like being watched?

Not that way.

What way?

(She shrugs her shoulders.)

Do you feel threatened by it?

You could put it that way.

What way do you put it?

That way is good enough.

The cat had been lying on the white velvet chaise longue like a patch of night. Black on white—a striking contrast. To anyone else it would have appeared to be resting. We knew that it was waiting. Or rather, lying in wait. I sensed her growing agitation, which I shared. It stared at us with uncanny malevolent eyes, its sharp claws gripping and releasing, gripping and releasing the soft, plump upholstery of the chaise. It stared at us, and the daylight seeped from the room. The buttercup pattern on the wallpaper, the ruffled yellow cover on the canopied bed, the embroidered pillows, the elegantly gowned dolls on their corner shelf—everything turned to shadows.

When I use the term *objective reality,* I refer to that reality which exists outside of our heads. I once had a patient, for example, who suffered great anxiety whenever her husband went away on a business trip. Regardless of the fact that he was a careful man, was not undertaking anything dangerous, and had, in the past, always returned safely, she was afraid for him each time he left. Now, there is usually an element of cause at the heart of our so-called neurotic fears. That is to say, what we fear is not entirely impossible. But it is highly unlikely. In the case of the woman, it was highly unlikely that her husband would not return as always. In other words, it was not an objective reality that she feared.

I suppose you are telling me, Doctor, that in all objective likelihood there is no such thing as a demonic cat.

The cat had jumped in through her window onto the chaise longue. The disturbing thing was that her room, on the third floor, was easily thirty feet from the ground. Since there were no trees outside the window that it might have climbed, the question remains: how did the cat get up there?

When I dream about cats, the dream always turns into a nightmare sooner or later.

That's very interesting. Do you recall having used the word *nightmare* in reference to something else?

No.

"A nightmare in the heart"?

I don't remember.

It was your definition of spiritual love.

Sounds like something I might have said, all right. For shock value. I'm big on shock value.

Let's talk about cats. What do they mean to you? What do they represent?

She opened the bedroom door wide. She attempted to shoo the cat out of the room by waving her arms about its head in a quasi striking motion. Did she do this for my sake? I doubt that she would have done it for herself alone. She was not in the habit of demanding anything for herself. Still, how we affect or disaffect one another is not always as clear and simple as it appears to be on the surface. I did know in advance that her efforts to be rid of the thing would prove futile. Yet I did not stop her.

Cats. I thought of them as beautiful. As warm. As the source of uncompromising love. The usual crap. They didn't represent a damned thing other than nice little pets until they started turning up in nightmares. Until they started doing kind of nightmarish things.

Such as?

Eating me up.

Oh? In your nightmares they ate you up?

Yes. Starting at the cunt and going on from there until there was nothing left.

So, you would say that the threat they represent is sexual in nature?

You would say that. I don't see anything sexy about being dinner for a cannibalistic cat.

Let's talk a little about nightmares. Cat nightmares and nightmares of the heart.

Another cat might have jumped down and run off. This one watched her appraisingly and continued to claw the velvet chaise as if to say . . .

I read you, Doctor. Cats are to guilt as sex is to original sin. That is what you want me to say, isn't it?

If that is what you think.

What I think is that these little stories we're telling each other are a whole lot of bullshit.

In desperation she grabbed it by the neck and ran with it out to the stairway—a wide, balustraded stairway, dizzying to peer down. The cat clung to her wildly, raking both of her arms bloody—the flesh in places hung in strips—before she was able to shake it off and see it fall, shrieking, to the polished-parquet floor below. Not three minutes later it stood at the doorway of her room.

On your first visit here we talked briefly about fear. I'd like to go back to that a bit. To what the things are that you find frightening.

Suppose I were to tell you *the world*, Doctor. Suppose I were to say that the entire world is a turn off?

Then I'd have to ask you to be more specific since we can't get too far dealing in generalities. Of what, in the world, are you afraid?

With a cry, she sprang to the door. She caught the animal between door and door jamb and threw her weight against it. It slipped in effortlessly, apparently uninjured, padded across the room, leaped onto the chaise that still bore the slight imprint of its earlier clawing, and settled itself with imperious indifference in the same spot it had occupied before.

I'm afraid of not being liked. By anyone at all, I mean. Both people who matter to me and people who don't. Which doesn't make any sense, does it? Why should I care about being liked by people who don't matter to me?

What does it mean to you to be liked?

(The hum of the air conditioner gets suddenly louder and then softer again as she begins to speak.)

That I'm good.

And not to be liked?

That I'm bad.

What you are saying, then, is that being liked is being assured of your goodness, being assured of your intrinsic worth. What we must work on is that you start liking yourself independently of others. That you take very deliberate steps to start liking yourself.

But I can like myself. I can feel great just by telling them to go fuck themselves with a barber pole. I can get a rush just seeing their faces slam shut to me like doors. And at the same time I can be sick over it. Ready to kill myself over it.

Would you say that one part of you is in conflict with the other part?

(The air conditioner's hum gets louder again. A rattle develops in it. She shifts on the leather couch, first crossing, then uncrossing her legs. Her skirt, which she has carefully kept pulled down up to now, rides up above her knees. A sardonic grin enlivens her features.)

I would say that the line of demarcation between body and soul has grown indistinct. I may be wrong, of course. The flesh may have been an integral part of the spirit all along. Or, to put it more simply, the soul and the asshole may always have been made of the same clay.

She had always been so pleasant, so obedient. As a child she never gave them a minute of worry, they said. Then, inexplicably, she changed. First there was the cat incident, which she refused to discuss. This cat that she suddenly couldn't bear to have in the same room had been her pet, her love upon which she had lavished innumerable kisses and pats, catnip mice, lit-

tle balls that tinkled when they rolled across the floor, and so on. She changed from one day to the next. She began to have brief and terrible love affairs during which she might be gone from the house all night or for several days, returning disheveled and frequently bearing bruises, whip marks, or bites on her body. These affairs lasted a week on the average, two weeks at the most. One morning she would just wake up listless, seemingly cured of her passion. They'd begin to hope she had come back to them. And then she would fall in love again.

You tell me you're afraid of not being liked, and yet you choose men who don't behave very lovingly toward you. Can we talk about that?

What do you want to hear?

We can start with what you actually want for yourself, what you are looking for. Because, as I suppose you're aware, there are distinct contradictions between what you say and what you do.

No, I'm not aware of that. In fact, I don't agree with it.

Yesterday, if I understood you correctly, you said that you could feel both exhilarated and sickened by the same behavior, the same act. Aren't those contradictory reactions?

You assume, Doctor, that our innermost feelings can be communicated in words. I've found out they can't. Very little of what we say gets through to anyone. Which is why pain tells much more than hugs and kisses. A scream more than a sigh. A kick in the head more than any fond little pat.

Would you say that love is getting kicked?

I used to hate myself because I was lonely. Because I was sad. Because I was readily ignored. I hated my body because people seemed to see through it or around it. I hated my mind for being locked in my body.

They criticized her. Threatened her. Suffered because of her. Stopped speaking to her. Started speaking again. Stopped again. They found her black-leather-bound diary, picked the lock, read it, and were horrified. They confronted her with their horror. She told them that horror was in the eye of the beholder.

As a child I was quiet and kept to myself. The idea was: if I am neither seen nor heard, I can't be hated.

Did you have any reason to believe you would be hated?

A very good reason. I picked a daisy. Daisies are supposed to tell, you know: one petal for yes, one petal for no. The last petal turned out to be a no. So all the possible future yeses were tainted in advance.

She had been walking along the river, a seedy area of dim bars and soot-darkened buildings. A low rail separated the street from the river. This filthy water flows into the ocean, she thought, and wondered if it became cleaner then or if, little by little, it polluted the sea. A flaccid condom, translucent as a jellyfish, bobbed near the oily surface. Her unexpected lover was only a voice warning her not to struggle or scream. He was only hands at her throat and a strong body pressing her against the rail, forcing her to bend over. He was stone-hardness against her naked skin. He was an urgent, furious, skewering embrace. She wanted to plead with him not to hurt her but her mouth, opening, filled up with his fury. When he was finished, he left her. A few days later she went looking for him. Since he had neither face nor name, her search was successful. She found him over and over, his face always masked like an executioner's, his hands always gloved, his powerful torso bare and gleaming. Each night she spent with him sickened her. Each night she spent with him deepened her longing to be annihilated in his embrace, extinguished against a body so beautiful, so much larger and stronger than her own.

I am at a complete loss for answers, Doctor.

I cannot swear to the accuracy of the following dialogue. I was not present when it originally took place. Neither was she. It falls, therefore, into the category of hearsay and may have suffered the usual distortions of interpretation.

It's as though she's a completely different person. I would really like to understand where I made my mistake. She was always such a good girl.
It's not a question of your mistake.
Certainly I must have done something terribly wrong for her to become like this. I always wanted the best for her. No one ever loved a child more than I loved her. Nor was as ill rewarded as I have been.
It's not a question of your mistake.
I was a teacher. I had exceptionally good rapport with my students. Every one of them. They came to me with whatever problems they had. I was always able to help them. Which is why it's exceptionally ironic that with her . . .
It's not a question of your mistake.
My husband doesn't get along with her particularly well. Hasn't for years. He's a businessman. Iron willed and immensely critical and demanding. He doesn't believe in giving praise, not even to me. I've spent a good part of my life preparing dinners for him that he's eaten without a word of thanks. Without a word, period. I have to carry the conversation throughout our dinners or we'd be eating in complete silence. Of course he is worried about her. In his way. He doesn't verbalize his disappointments. He keeps them to himself. He was disappointed when she was born because he wanted a son. Naturally. He got that from his father, who was a devil. A regular devil: selfish, inconsiderate, mean.
It's not a question of your mistake but of devils.
It's the bad seed. I've told him that. He has passed on the bad seed. The fault lies squarely in his lap. Of course he doesn't want to know about that. So he pretends not to hear.

It's not a question of your mistake but of how to exorcise devils.

In order for an exorcism to be staged there must be some short preliminary scenes: The Possessed sitting on the edge of the bed swinging her leg.

We are such *nice* people, you and I. So civilized. So loving . . .

The Possessed with fear hunched inside her like a troll hunched inside a hollow tree.

. . . that you have kept me on a leash all these years just not to lose me. And I have trotted at your heels all these years just not to get lost.

The Possessed picking up a hand mirror.

Look at me. I've half choked to death on your goddamned leash!

The Possessed flinging the hand mirror which shatters with a human scream, breaking the scene into blinding fragments. Blackout. Then a spotlight snaps on. It glares through a broken slat in a shuttered window. It illuminates a brass bed, the only furniture. This setting resembles a monastic cell in its white-walled barrenness. It also resembles a room that might once have been used for storage. The door is locked from the outside. She is lying on the bed. She tosses from right to left, from stomach to back. She lies still. We sense his approach across a swiftly diminishing distance. That sharpening scent of his anger stings like thousands of poisoned thorns. Though she cannot see what is happening offstage, she has periodic seizures of uncontrollable trembling. Offstage he is walking up the path to the house, coming to a halt in front of the door, ringing the bell. Offstage he is entering the house, standing in the vestibule beneath the heavy, burnished chandelier, talking to the others. Offstage he is ascending the spiral staircase. His hand grips the smooth rail of the balustrade as if for grimly needed support. (This slight sign of his weakness gives me a pang.) The tumblers turn in the lock. The door opens. He steps into the set. We are struck by the heat pouring off him and by the seductive pain-thrill of his hate. He approaches her without hesitation. He has come prepared with ropes. She is too stunned by fright and the staggering heat to struggle as he ties her arms and legs to the brass frame of the bed. I, dead calm as I always am in desperate straits, observe him with critical objectivity. He has dressed most seductively for the occasion: executioner's mask, black gloves, bare chest, silver-studded belt, black tights defining his virile loins. Seduction is his forte. He has reduced many an ambivalent lover to jelly merely with his superbly modulated voice.

Who are you?

His question is no more than a mellifluent purr.

Right now, I am an admirer.

He repeats the question more firmly, his voice subtly edged with rage. She jerks against the ropes. He is bestial and glorious. One could fall in love with the ferocity in his eyes, their sheen of fury, the sharp line of his jaw, each muscular curve of his body, each intake of breath.

Who are you?

He persists. He persists and his words cut like whips. She twists and writhes against her bonds, simultaneously murmuring acquiescence.

How many of you are there?

He persists. As though he were not just playing a part. As though beauty did not also contain the grotesque. As though nightmares were not, by definition, dreams. As though each of our shadows did not cast some light into another's darkness. As though there were such a thing as definitive answers. As though there were such a thing as answers rather than ever-burgeoning questions.

He that believeth and is baptized shall be saved; but he that believeth not shall be damned. And these signs shall follow them that believe and in my name shall they cast out devils.

He stands at the foot of the bed and touches his forehead and the left and right sides of his chest with the fingers of one gloved hand. Sweat beads his face. It runs in rivers down his chest. He raises his arms and douses her with his hot sweat that turns her pale flesh to bright pink. She moans, pleads, cries, shrieks with fever. His eyes, his maddened maddening eyes, transfix her as soundly as any gouging cock. Were she not tied, she would fling herself at him, crush herself to him, cover him completely.

I command you, ancient unclean serpent, to release this creature.

Were she not tied she would fling herself at his feet, wrap her arms around his legs, cover his thighs, his cock, his belly with her ravening mouth.

And he said unto them, I beheld Satan as lightning fall from heaven. Behold, I give unto you power to tread o: serpents.

But even tied as she is, her legs spread, her arms fastened above her head, her lacy robe falling open, her breath coming in short, low gasps, her sex richly glistening, she demands that he catch fire and burn—as we are burning. WE DEMAND THAT HE CATCH FIRE...

SECRETS

Some said J was truly beautiful. Others said she was quite ordinary looking but photographed well. J herself was ambivalent. She felt beautiful or ordinary or even ugly depending on whom she was with. When she asked her lover's opinion, he told her that, basically, he was into tits and asses, not faces.

"I wish you would be serious," she said. "What specifically turns you on about me?"

"The way you play with yourself," he said. "The way you move when you're coming."

In April she appeared on the cover of *Vogue* wearing a curly red wig over her straight brown hair. In May she appeared on the cover of *Glamour* wearing a blond afro. He began to insist on her wearing these wigs when they made love. She was twenty-nine years old and wondered what would happen to his love when she no longer appeared in magazines.

Her face, she decided, was too narrow. The cheekbones too insignificant. The eyes too close together. They had a frightened and, at the same time, dreaming look, as if focused on some distracting inner event.

She stood in front of the mirror in the small, unfamiliar bedroom and decided she had done the right thing in leaving. How many times had she longed for escape? To simply vanish from her existing life and appear somewhere else with a different name, a different history? Was it longing or fate that guided her to this place? It could not be an accident that she, who rarely read the paper, happened upon the ad:

TYPIST and related duties. Rare oppy
for right person. Reloc to mtn hideaway. Creative imagination a plus.

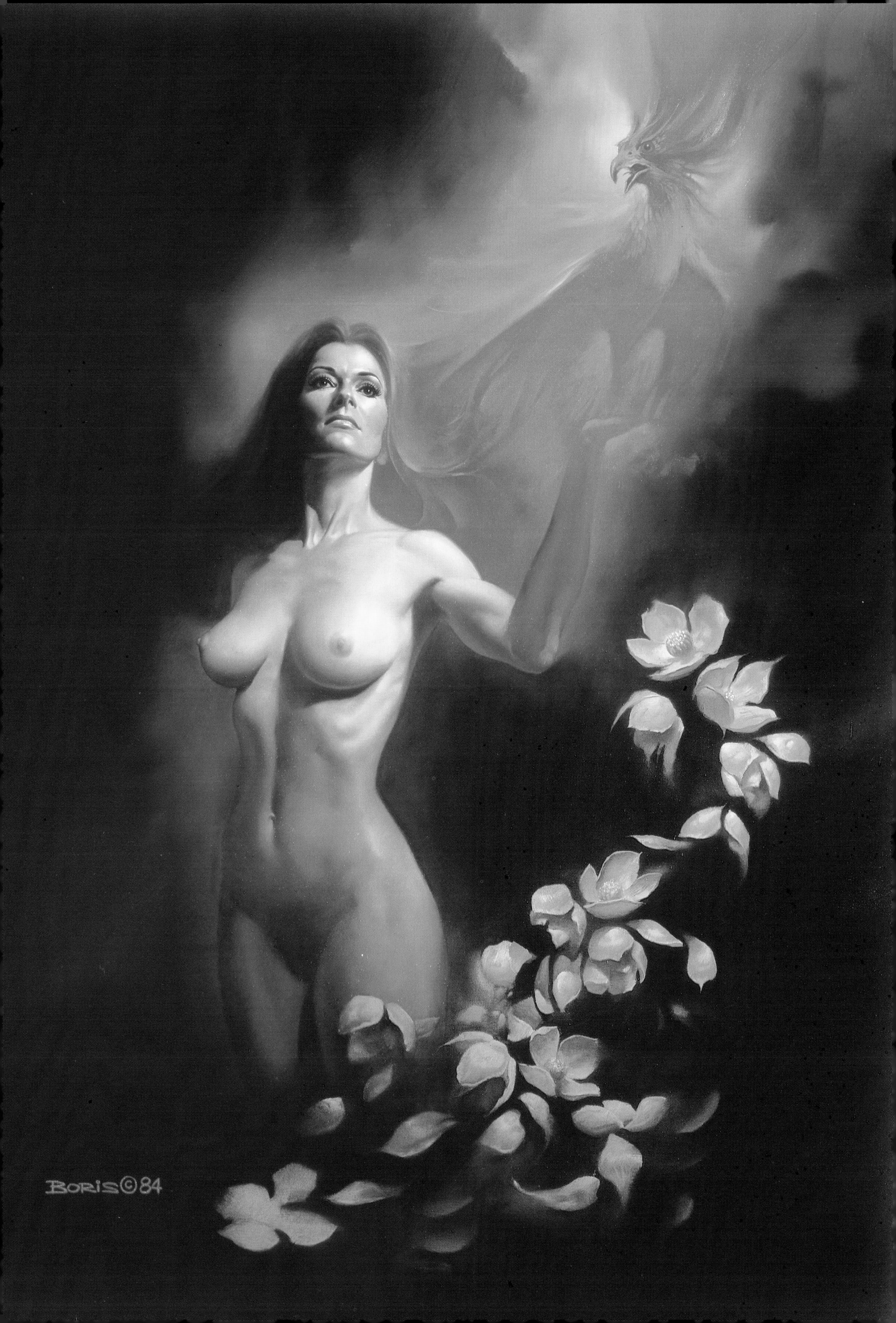
BORIS©84

"We want you to feel at home here, Juliana," the woman who hired her said.

Her lover would never find her here. Should he want to.

She had answered at once without the typical procrastination, the habitual agonizing *should I or shouldn't I?* that preceded every major move. That endless balancing of pros against cons became superfluous upon finding the card in her lover's jacket pocket (had he left it for her to find when he asked her to take the jacket to the cleaners?): a photograph of brilliantly colored balloons against a cerulean sky. And the message inside, written in a graceful looping script she did not recognize: *I love you a lot.*

The words had slammed into her heart like fists.

"If there's anything you need or want to know, don't hesitate to ask," the woman said. There was a sadness about her smile. As if she knew very well what it was to need and have no one to ask.

I love you a lot. The discovery came like a long-awaited foe, inevitable as death. So, here it is, J thought, putting the jacket down. She stood holding the card in her hand, waiting for tears to dissolve her, waiting for her legs to buckle, waiting to fall through the hole in her heart.

The card did not even quiver in her hand. And suddenly she hated him.

At least by refusing to confront him with the evidence of his betrayal she eliminated his ignominious lies in advance.

"Juliana," she said to herself with the air of someone checking the fit of a newly tailored coat. She believed in the protective properties of names. She had chosen Juliana not only because it bore no relation to her actual name but also to camouflage her sense of deficiency. This name had strength.

She studied "Juliana" with interest in the full-length mirror: tall, confident, elegant in her black skirt and high-necked blouse; long black lashes framing sea-green eyes in an aristocratic face unmarked by anguish. At least that, she thought. At least I can *look* like a Juliana. Her own face, superimposed on Juliana's, was, like the faintest of ghosts, barely visible. The trouble was with dreams from which she'd awaken with a start, unable, for a few terrible moments, to catch her breath. Her conscious mind had severed itself from certain images that still reverberated through her body and from which she would tear herself with a terrible effort, needing to run and not understanding where the danger lay.

The "mountain hideaway" was unlike anything J had imagined. With its somber brown shingles and slanted roof to which a rusted weather vane had been anchored, it appeared considerably smaller that it was. Perhaps the thick growth of trees crowding it on three sides aided the illusion of its size.

Whatever the cause of its deceptive outward appearance, the magnificence of the foyer took her by surprise: the gold walls, the chandelier gleaming with crystal, the marble statue of a young woman with a bird in her arms, the wine-carpeted stairway onto which the bright noon sun poured through a huge yellow-leaded glass window, dazzling sunlight that faded to whispering pastel shadows near the top of the stairs.

The effect of this and the high-ceilinged rooms (which, she was to discover, led in disorienting circles: sitting room, dining room, library, alcove, snaking off into what might be a servant's wing: pantry, kitchen, and, abruptly, from a new perspective, the foyer again) was to create a certain confusion, as in those dreams in which well-known streets and houses change subtly and perplexingly while the dreamer struggles with increasing anxiety against the admission of being lost.

"What a beautiful house this is," J said as she followed the woman up the stairs and along a poorly lit corridor. The walls, she noted, were marred by criss-crossing hair-thin cracks to which shadows clung like dust.

Her room, in fortunate contrast to the corridor, was light and pretty. It was furnished with a four-poster bed, a small marble-topped night table, an armchair, a mahogany chest of drawers, and a standing mirror. A watercolor hung on the wall directly above the bed. Its subject: a mass of trampled flowers. The splashes of reds, purples, greens were so vibrant, so alive as to give the impression of a luxuriant bouquet. Only when she stood directly in front of it (later, after the sun had moved and the air was markedly cooler) did she notice the barely inch-long stems jutting like broken bones out of the earth, and the ghostly imprint of shoes on the sumptuous petals.

If she stayed here any length of time, she thought, she would take the painting down. She could replace it with a large photograph. Perhaps. One of the more exciting ones from her portfolio. The nude superimposed on the blow-up of butterfly wings: J as a fairy-tale creature in flight, her arms raised above her head creating, at once, the suggestion of antennae and the gesture of supplication.

As she stood contemplating the trompe l'oeil effect of the watercolor flowers, a silvery laugh floated toward her from somewhere in the house.

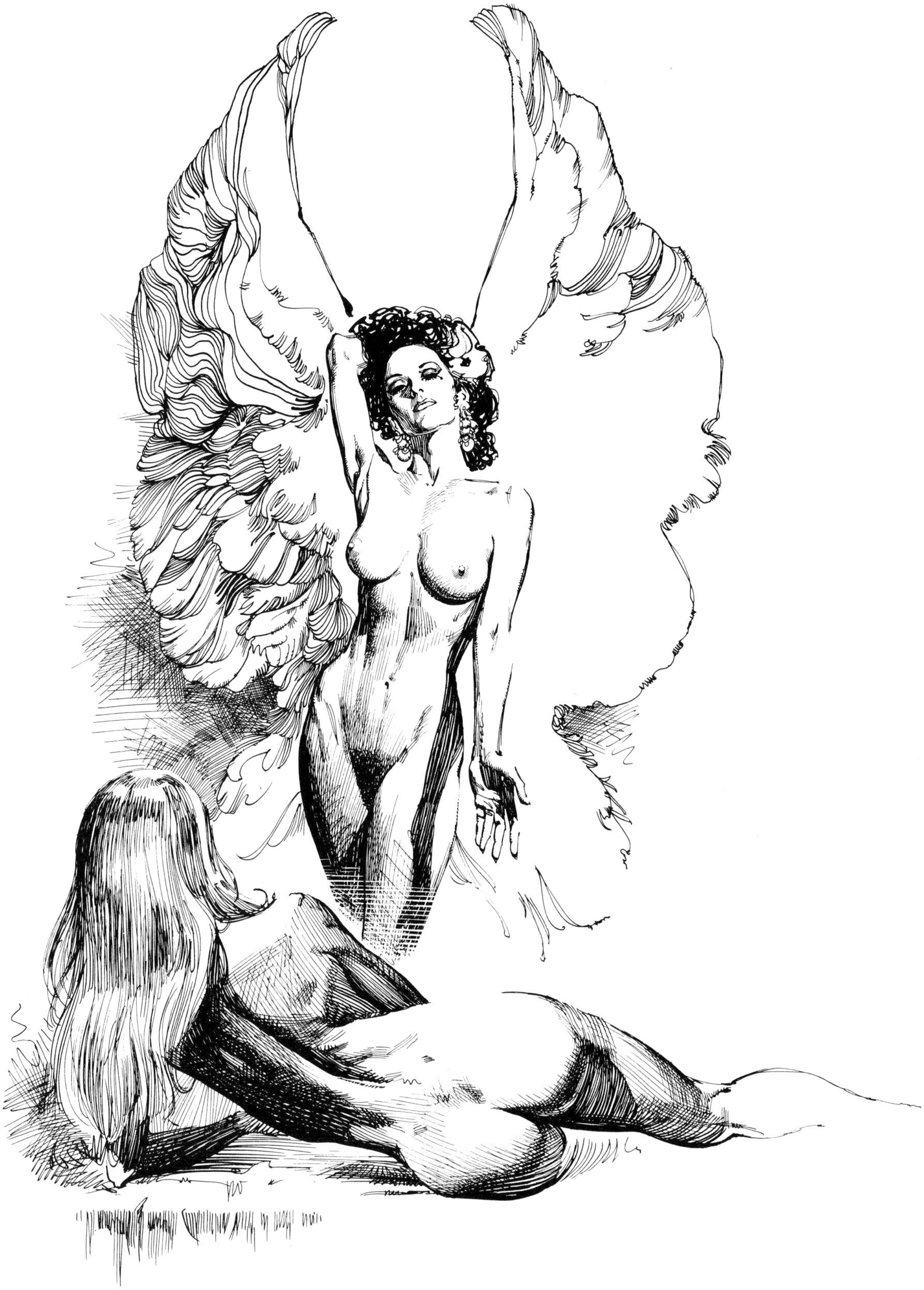

Breakfast was at 8:30. The aroma of buttered toast and coffee, fresh orange juice, scrambled eggs. Everything set out on a red-and-white checkered tablecloth —so welcoming. Why, then, her uneasiness? Because this place was new to her? Because changes always made her uneasy? Even necessary changes? Even changes for the better?

Her employer was a short man, roughly her own height. Small men invariably had big complexes. What were his? Stop it, she thought. No point in stockpiling negative ideas. He had a surprisingly sensual mouth in an otherwise stern, somehow angry face.

He leafed through the manuscript she would be typing and ate without seeming to taste his food. Alongside him the woman chatted breathlessly, her dialogue punctuated every so often by a nervous giggle: she had better pick up more butter, cheese, possibly a steak for dinner; the vegetable garden needed weeding; the plumber should be contacted (giggle) or the painter or possibly both, the plumber first and then the painter because surely it was a leak that caused the paint on the dining room ceiling to flake so badly (another giggle).

At the mention of the ceiling, the man shot her a coldly silencing look. Then, turning to J, he asked how long she expected the typing to take. There were exactly six hundred and twenty handwritten legal-size pages, he added.

"How is Juliana supposed to know how long it will take to finish when she hasn't begun yet?" the woman anxiously interceded. "She wasn't hired to predict the future, you know."

"Predictions of a certain nature are always possible to make," the man said, pointing at the platter of toast his wife automatically passed to him along with the butter. "The study of sociology, for instance, is based on the predictability of human behavior. Psychology as well. It is highly predictable, for example, that an individual who has learned to fear others will himself become frightening."

The woman laughed as if to minimize her husband's words, J thought. As if to defuse them. Then she rose, abruptly pushing back her chair, and suggested J type on the screened-in porch at the rear of the house where she would not be disturbed.

The trouble was with the incessant chirping of invisible birds, particularly one monotonous mechanical chirrup obstinately repeated every few seconds.

The trouble was that the manuscript itself set her mind to wandering. So, although she felt that she was typing diligently, she would catch herself not typing, catch herself just staring at the scrawl of words on the yellow-lined paper. She was enormously relieved, later on, when the man made no inquiries about her progress. Perhaps by having turned it over to her he had divested himself of all immediate connection with it?

The trouble was, she could not shake the sense that the manuscript was not a work of fiction at all. Neither could it be autobiography, however.

It was called *Quasimodo*. Yet the narrator bore no similarity whatever to Victor Hugo's hunchback.

The trouble was that her back began to ache intolerably after a while. Probably because she was not used to sitting stiffly erect at a typewriter for hours at a time.

QUASIMODO

I have lived in this drafty, inhospitable house all my life. Often enough I plotted escape, but lacked the freedom of spirit to act. When my parents were alive, their need of me moored me to the place. After they died I could find no buyer for it, consequently lacked the funds to leave and gradually gave up the hope if not the desire to do so. Now, when I pass through the huge domed room where they used to sit in front of the fire on winter evenings, I occasionally hear their repudiating voices. The sorrow I caused and still cause them echoes throughout the place.

It is true that I have let things go to seed. The roof leaks. Broken windowpanes have not been replaced. Generations of spiders have festooned the ceilings and doorways with their spookish lacework. A storm wind hissing through cracks in the walls might be the panting of monsters.

I try to tell them it isn't entirely my fault. The needed repairs are too costly and, by now, too extensive. In addition, I feel that I am a stranger here and, as such, not obliged to sink my little bit of money into the place. And yet, this rotting mansion with its hidden stairways, its secret rooms, its inaccessible towers and gables, is the place of my exile.

I understand that I have committed inexpiable crimes, though what they were, I have forgotten. I understand that there is such a thing as enduring guilt. I do not resent my loneliness which, insulating and familiar, blankets me like burial earth gently heaped upon a coffin. Hourly it whispers its comforting, annihilating dirge.

I might have simply surrendered to my loneliness, embraced it, been content to wander aimlessly through an eternally frozen landscape, trusted the justness of my sentence. But one day I discovered what, perhaps, was never meant for me to know. Should I say that it terrified me? That it seduced me? Is the discovery of night terrifying? Can one fall in love with the intangible? with shadows?

It had been raining for days, a gray drizzle alternating with a heavy, pelting downpour. I'd built a fire in the stone hearth of the domed room in order to mitigate the dampness that had settled like a dull pain into my bones. I'd lost track of how long I sat there gazing into the flames. The crackle of burning wood was a muted singsong in my ears. I imagined the yellow flames to have a sentient life, to be some form of otherworldly intelligence dancing on the glowing snapping logs, singing to me in their odd, wispy voices.

Yes, I pretended that they were not just singing but singing to me. And I understood them in the way that a quiescent sea urchin might understand the pull of the tide. I closed my eyes and found their beckoning shapes, impressed on my retinas, more brilliant and dazzling even than in reality.

When the fire began to burn low, I arose to get more logs. Having sat in one position for too long, I was able to straighten up only with considerable pain. Getting old, I thought to myself with a vaguely regretful sense of loss. It was when I turned that I noticed the peculiar markings on the floor behind me: tiny scratch marks. I got down (not without discomfort) on all fours to examine them. It struck me as highly peculiar that I had not noticed them before. Thin, fresh scratchings on the old wood. Even more remarkable was the trail of minute paw prints in the patina of dust. As if some small clawed animal had been prancing in ever-widening circles. The prints suddenly veered off in a straight line through the doorway to the outer hall. There, due to the paucity of light, I could not follow them.

It is perfectly clear to me now that I might have dismissed this business without repercussions. Had I been less lonely, less weighted by the grueling monotony of my life, I might have said: "These are mouse tracks," thus logically divesting my discovery of both terror and romance. I did have the choice. And yet I wonder to what extent our choices are predetermined by our genes.

I rummaged through the long-neglected clutter in the pantry and netted eight partly burned candles. These I affixed to a warped cutting board, fashioning a crude candelabra with which I was able to pick up the mysterious trail once again. On my knees, and with my face barely inches from the dirt-veined floor, I followed the tracks up four flights of stairs to the low-ceilinged top of the house. My parents had used this floor for storage. It was to this spot that broken chairs, a trunk with rusting lock and hinges, moldering clothes, part of a croquet set, and similar relics had all been consigned and forgotten. An attic crawlspace (which may or may not have originally been meant

for storage) was accessible through a three-foot-square trapdoor in the ceiling. To the best of my knowledge it had never been used. It had no actual floor, I was told, only exposed beams. Whoever should be imprudent enough to climb up into it (which I was expressly forbidden to do) risked, at the very least, a serious fall.

Far from being curious as a child, I experienced an intense aversion to it. I would no sooner have investigated than lit black candles to invoke the devil. I do seem to recall having been up there once with my mother and hearing a soft fluttering sound which she attributed to bats, a congregation of bats nesting in the crawlspace.

As I stood there again with my makeshift candelabra, I saw that the trapdoor had been sealed with a heavy padlock. What year this was done or where the key might be, I have no idea. The cobwebs spun (as if for additional security) across it might have been undisturbed for centuries. Except...

One silky filament had been recently broken.

The trail of tiny inhuman tracks led unerringly up the wall, across the ceiling, and ended at this spot. The trap door itself had not been moved. The thing I'd followed appeared to have slipped between the door and the thick frame into which the door was set. Yet the tracks, small as they were, indicated something too large for this maneuver.

Fresh flowers had been set on the table for lunch, which took place on the patio, a flagstoned area walled in by trees, a grape arbor, and the back of the house. The table had been set with blue dishes, blue scalloped napkins, polished silver, a platter of assorted cold cuts and cheeses, and a basket of rolls.

As had been the case at breakfast, the man appeared preoccupied and largely oblivious to J while the woman prattled on with breathless energy, her conversation seemingly directed at no one in particular. Occasionally she would pause and look at J, who would then stammer a sort of answer to disguise the fact that she had only been half listening.

"It's really quite fascinating," she said to some question concerning the manuscript and, to lend this answer more validity, asked the man where he got his ideas from.

"From my head," he answered.

The woman laughed and (so it seemed to J) glanced at one of the upper windows.

J would have resumed her work immediately after lunch, but the weather had turned uncomfortably warm. Her long-sleeved blouse was soaked through with perspiration and she decided to change into lighter clothes.

No doubt it was the bright daylight on the patio that accounted for the seeming darkness inside the house, the illusion that the rooms, increased in size, had shifted locations. She was certain it had been the kitchen that led to the patio. Instead it was the dining room she entered from there and in which she seemed to see the statue of the woman with the bird that she knew quite well stood in the foyer. Of course the statue turned out not to be there, only her own shadow cast on the opposite wall. And, of course, there must be more than one entrance from the patio into the house.

As soon as her eyes adjusted to the reduced light, she found her way to the stairs and back to her room.

She closed the door behind her and knew that someone had been there. The window, which she had left closed, was wide open, and a heavy, somnolent heat poured thickly into the room. She closed it again with some difficulty because the latch had been painted over innumerable times and did not turn readily. Once she succeeded in locking it, however, the room did gradually get cooler. Now the branches of a tree brushed against the milky glass, the leaves, like dark fingers, softly tapping a coded warning.

A dull throb, more like a heartbeat than an ache, had begun in her head. She moved toward the bed. Perhaps, before tackling the afternoon's work, she should lie down a bit. Not long. Fifteen minutes should be enough to revive her. Slipping off her shoes, she lay down and stretched to relieve the tension in her body.

The stirring leaves cast shadows into the room that became intensely black in some areas. As, for instance, in the mirror. An opaque black shadow glimmered metallically in the mirror. Another optical illusion, obviously. If she got up again to confirm this, however, she might as well forget about her nap. On the other hand, if she waited...

She stood directly in front of the shadow. Would it reach out and touch her? contaminate her? It was close enough. Rather than step back out of its reach, she closed her eyes. It was still there, imprinted on the retinas. She opened her eyes.

It was there, ebony black, light glancing like daggers off its polished surfaces: a statue with firm, uptilted breasts, tapered waist, rounded hips. With a slow, insinuating gesture, the statue raised its hand. It held something in its hand. A bird. A black bird with a touch of red to its breast. The red flickered like dancing sparks. The statue held something in its hand. A red bird. Fire red. It spread its fire-red wings and fluttered in her hand like a fire dancing. The fire leaped up the length of her arm; it licked at her neck. The statue raised her burning arm in a slow, insinuating gesture.

J, facing her, mimicked the gesture. J, too, held something in her hand. A bird, cold as a stone, with fire-red feathers. The feathers grew, not just on the bird, but also on J's hand. There was no distinction between where the bird ended and J's hand began. The feathers grew redly up her arm to form a blood-red strangling ruff at her neck.

The trouble was with dreams.

From which she invariably awakened with a start, her heart racing as if to outrun her.

She lay on the bed and looked at the ceiling. She thought of her lover. It was for him, for his admiration, for his approval that she had exhausted herself running to endless interviews, endless shootings, endlessly smiling into the camera—those great exuberant smiles that left her cheeks aching. Her life for their ten years together had been one long race toward his approval, one long thrust toward his love.

And all he required, in his own words, were "tits and ass." Nothing like overshooting the mark, she thought bitterly. She thought of his penis: upright, turgid with expectation, fiercely, exquisitely primed for the fuck. It still had the power to excite her. *It*, she thought, one hand moving smoothly across her body, softly between her thighs. *It and not he.*

She had left him.

She had been the one to leave.

That was important to keep in mind.

But she'd left with the desperation of the dying.

He had begun to look at her with distaste. After the accident. After the day she set a pot of water on the stove, exactly as she had done thousands of times. Only this time the flame burst from the jet, ignited the cuff of her robe and, in an instant, the entire sleeve. She'd torn the robe off and stamped out the flames, but her arm, her shoulder and, part of her neck had been burned. The burns left scars.

"I'd have had to stop modeling anyway one of these years," she told her lover. "I'll just begin something new a bit sooner than I'd planned."

She had always been interested in photography and had a good feeling for it, a good visual imagination. That, then, seemed to be the direction to go in. She invested in an Olympus, a Hasselblad, and four thousand dollars worth of lenses. She rented a studio. She thought it might be a better idea to open her own modeling agency. She put an ad in *Show Business* and spent several weeks interviewing prospective models. She weighed the pros and cons of each career regularly, but a peculiar uneasiness anchored her to indecision.

Possibly she only imagined that he avoided looking at her. She took care not to appear entirely naked in front of him. Not to leave the scars exposed. Was it her self-consciousness that broadened the distance between them?

In the room above hers there was a sound. The creak of bed springs? Someone making love? Not her employers, surely. Surely...?

She sat up and swung her legs over the side of the bed. Six feet away, in the mirror, her image also sat up, awake and on guard. "I must get back to work," she said to invisible ears.

My instinct was to investigate no further; to ascribe this unsettling business to imagination coupled with a capricious trick of the light. However, it was already too late. I had seen something I should not have seen, stumbled on something forbidden. I was unpleasantly reminded of a recurrent dream in which I discover a trapdoor in the floor of the cellar. It apparently leads to a subcellar. I am determined to pry up this door despite a strong and unaccountable sense of dread. I labor at it for a while. I am beginning to feel, with relief, that I will not get it open after all, when it creaks slowly open on its own. Rotting stairs lead down into absolute darkness. I hold my lantern over the opening and see nothing. I sense rather than hear something moving in the darkness. Suddenly a cold wind blasts up out of the hole and extinguishes my lantern. I awake thoroughly chilled and shaken. I always awake before discovering what is down there.

Yes, that was a dream. But the reality was not far removed. An uncanny creature co-existed with me under this roof. I sensed danger in its proximity. The evidence of its existence was an admonition traversing the years. Had the creature always lived here? Had I been the one to padlock the trapdoor and conveniently erase the act from my memory?

I did not break the lock and climb into the crawl-space. I did not arm myself against it. I knew that I had to keep up the pretense of its unimportance. I had to prevent it from becoming too real.

J was not at all surprised when, over dinner, the woman announced their plans to spend the weekend with friends.

"I hope you don't mind being alone here, Juliana," she said.

The news materialized so naturally out of the mood set by the manuscript she was typing, it struck her as inevitable. As if, from the moment she saw the ad in the paper, she was fated to end up alone in this strange house where it would not be at all remarkable to find footprints tracking up a bare wall to a door.

"No, I don't mind," J said. It was useless to speculate on the vagaries of fate. "Is there anything I should know? Anyone who might call?"

"Not a thing," the woman said.

The man said nothing.

Somewhere above them in the house there was a tapping sound—almost, J thought, like Morse code.

She opened her eyes to the sound of their voices. Were they in the room next to hers? Below hers? Above hers? The house played desultory acoustical tricks. Were they fighting? The woman's voice, uncharacteristically strident, sounded like hammer blows. The man's was no more than a murmur. She couldn't hear what they were saying, only the sound of it: hammer blows, hammer blows, and then the submissive murmurs. Were they making love?

She opened her eyes to the sound of a silvery laugh floating toward her from somewhere above.

She opened her eyes to the sound of a car motor starting. Dawn lit the rectangle of her window. So, they were leaving already. She should have been up to see them off. To wish them a good weekend. She should, at least, go to the window and wave to them. She should overcome this paralyzing weakness and go...

She opened her eyes to the sound of something in the room. A woman sat on the edge of her bed. Or what appeared to be a woman. Her skin, the color of lilacs, emitted a lilac scent. It might have been the rustle of her wings that had awakened J.

"What do you want?" J asked, noting, as the woman began to stroke her legs, that they were uncovered. The long purple talons made a hissing sound against her skin.

It occurred to J that she might be asleep and dreaming this. She had not, after all, asked, "Who are you?" which should have been the first thing to ask. *Who are you*—to indicate that she was talking to a real person and not to a phantom.

"Who are you?" she said.

The woman leaned over her, her long, scented hair sweeping silken and soft as a spider's web against J's cheek.

"Juliana," the woman breathed, taking J's face between her weirdly beautiful beastlike hands, pressing her lips against J's lips, parting them slightly, tracing their shape with her virile tongue.

Lilacs were falling, falling, covering J completely. She lay crushed beneath them. She lay coldly barricaded beneath them. Her heart was beating too strongly for this to be a dream. The hiss of talons against her skin was too loud. She waited beneath her barricade. Something fleshy forced its way into her. Something wriggled and turned inside her. Something with a little flamelike tongue that slowly, slowly began to melt her.

The woman took J in her arms, lifting her out of the lilac mist, stroking her liquid neck and breasts, her pubic mound. Her enchanted fingers went in and out, in and out, filling J with flower petals. She kissed

J's eyelids, her lips, her nipples, her belly, her clitoris, and the soft furrow between her buttocks. She beautified her with kisses. She caressed all the darkness and all the shadows out of her.

J opened her eyes to a sound somewhere above her. She gazed at the mosaic of fine cracks in the yellowing ceiling. She thought the texture of the ceiling was much like the meticulously powdered skin of an aging face. Sunlight streamed through the window. Clearly the morning was almost gone.

"Are you happy with me?" she once asked her lover.

"What's happy?" he said. "If I had a million bucks I wouldn't be happy because I'd be chasing after the second million."

There was a sound somewhere above her. A door opening?

"I hope this photography business of mine will get off the ground," she'd said when it seemed likely that the model agency would not.

"Hope is nice," her lover said. "And so is faith and charity. But you still gotta have ninety cents to get on the subway."

Clearly the morning was almost gone, and she had no idea how. Only the sense of something forgotten, something of fundamental importance.

The morning was almost gone when she sat up in bed, her heart pounding. She had to investigate the upper floor of the house, and a formless dread weighted her as she rose, put on a robe, walked to the door, and opened it.

The corridor became longer and narrower as she advanced. Silence leaned toward her from every doorway. It hung in corners. It eddied around the bends. Where she had expected to find a flight of stairs, the open door of an empty room only led to another corridor. The silence was broken by the sound of a window opening. A breeze sprang up. It tugged lightly at her robe. The smell of fresh lilacs beckoned her.

She discovered a stairwell hidden away in a shadowy nook. She might have passed without noticing it except that the scent of lilacs grew particularly

strong there. As she started up the stairs, the shadows deepened. Halfway along, a piece of plaster broke from the old wall and fell to bits at her feet. The small white chunks of plaster looked like dead moths scattered on the dark wood. An instant later, they stirred, revived, fluttered past her astonished face and were gone up the stairwell. A laugh—like the twittering of excited birds—floated from above.

Giddiness rocked her. She thought she would fall, but the moment passed. She had better hurry. The silence, which had momentarily receded, was already uncoiling, closing in. She ran up the few remaining stairs and stepped out onto a small, square landing. The graying day filtered through a cobwebbed skylight.

Dust coated the wooden floor. It outlined the cracks and pockmarks on the walls. Closed doors on every side. No sign of the moths. No clue to where they might be. Where anyone might be. No prints in this dust. Nothing. Only silence moving softly in corners. Silence thrumming like an anxious heart.

And then a silvery laugh behind the door directly across from her. Or not a laugh, but the twittering of a bird?

She approached on tiptoe, careful not to make the floor creak beneath her feet. She stood outside the closed door and listened. Silence. And the pulsation of bated breath. She turned the knob slowly.

The room, a lady's room, bright with sunlight (so it couldn't be that late after all), was amazingly similar to her own. The four-poster bed, the marble-topped night table, the painting above the bed (only in this one the flowers, vividly alive, had not been trampled on), the large standing mirror turned so that it caught her wondering image framed in the doorway. For an instant she thought it was someone else, a stranger, a woman with rustling wings and a cloud of hair.

Clothes had been laid out on the white chenille bedspread: lace underwear, a silk high-necked blouse with puffy sleeves, a pretty black slightly flared skirt. She approached the bed, untied the sash of her robe, slipped it off, and, one by one, put on the new things. They fit perfectly.

VOYEUR

. . . the slight movement of her sheer curtains, the notes of a Ravel sonata drifting in from the next room, the sunlight flecking her warm, bare skin with gold. She savors the caress of the sun. She has no idea how closely I watch her. Or how time goes gray and passes in a haze when she is gone. But I can await her return with patience. I have gotten used to a life that offers little more than long periods of sleep. My existence, for almost a century and a half, unfolded largely behind closed doors with only the gathering dust for company.

What can I say about us? How describe our connection with each other? To say we have never exchanged a word is to imply that we are strangers. To say we are lovers is to destroy a fragile truth by reducing it to finite terms.

She is oblivious to my adoration which, far from diminishing our relationship, enhances it. I am privileged to see her as no one else can, not her friends, not her husband, not the lovers she takes from time to time. I alone witness all her moods, her flavors, her poses, her changes. Only I enjoy her as intensely as any lover and yet am safe from her deceptions. She presents herself to me without guile, without artifice or pretense. At times she stands so near me I can breathe her perfume. Yet she is, very nearly, unaware of my presence.

. . . the whisperings of her curtains at my shoulder, the sensuous murmur of music, the kisses of sunlight, the slight thrust of her pelvis against her hand, her teasing fingers, the tension of the muscles in her legs—particularly her right leg. Her breathing changes. Her mouth opens slightly as if she suddenly needs more air, a need also signaled in her closed eyes, the lids of which squeeze together tightly for the quivering breath of a moment.

I absorb her shiver, her accelerating pulse, the increasing pressure of her fingers against her flesh and—all at once—the stillness. Sometimes I watch only the changes in her breathing. Sometimes only her face, her eyes, her mouth. Sometimes only her hands: where she touches herself and how and, at

52

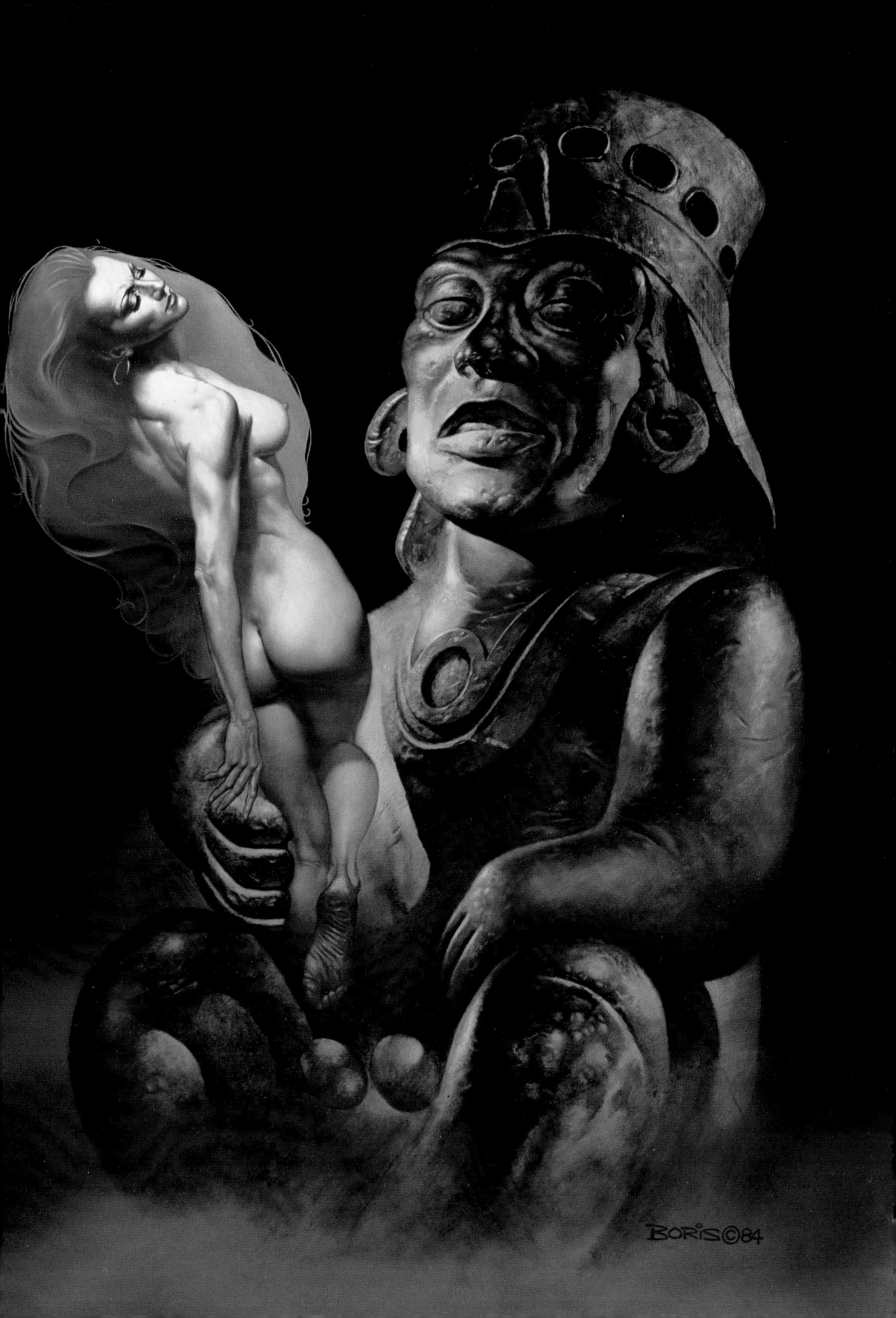
BORIS©84

the end, how her left hand will tense suddenly and then go limp.

Her cat, a silky black and white persian, jumps up on the bed, approaches her on stalking feet, halts, thrusts its arch little face straight into her bush, and withdraws, shaking its head to shake off invisible moisture. It flicks a pink tongue across its whiskered mouth. At that instant I too can taste her.

The cat jumps lightly over her thigh to curl up in the inviting hollow of her waist and hip. She begins to stroke it absently.

My face never changes. It bears, I believe, an expression of delight. I have never seen it. For centuries I have only looked straight ahead, never back at myself. My self-awareness, such as it is, has evolved through things others have said about me, through their behavior in relation to me, their rituals in which I played a silent though integral part.

Long ago, if I remember correctly, I was a kind of god.

Her lover is younger than she. She has chosen him for his youth, his sensuous mouth and straight, chiseled nose, his broad chest and the hard swell of his biceps, but, above all, for the love-struck solicitousness that makes him accept all the little torments she visits on him.

"Our relationship really does not have a future," she tells him as they are about to make love. She says this with the sweetest of sad smiles. It excites her to tantalize him, to urge his step by step approach as she measuredly retreats.

"Don't talk like that," he says, taking her in his arms. He is a struggling writer. Not without talent, she believes. He is writing a novel of which she is the tragic romantic heroine. When it is finished she plans to show it to a friend of her husband's who is a literary agent. Yet, regardless of what happens then, she thinks it will probably take him years to make real money. If he ever does.

"It wouldn't be right to make any promises to you," she says, "that I won't or can't keep. Because I do love you. Because I don't want there to be any lies between us. It would be dishonest of me to pretend that I plan to leave him. Or, for that matter, to leave any of this." Her gesture includes the house, the surrounding gardens, the swimming pool and cabana, the tennis court, and her small red Mercedes parked beside it. "But that doesn't have to stop us from enjoying each other now, while we're together," she adds, tightening her legs around him, crossing her ankles at the small of his back.

The interweaving of his tanned body with her paler

one blends these two into a single exotic entity; they could be a rare jungle plant rocking and trembling in the strange cannibal act of devouring itself. There is a species of flora native to South Africa that, in times of drought, absorbs its own leaves in order to grow. I imagine it looking like these two fused in the act of making love. However, I don't know for certain. I've never seen it.

She gazes at him appraisingly as he dresses. She decides that he reminds her of Michelangelo's David. She draws in her abdomen, arches slightly, props her head on one hand, and momentarily banishes all the telltale softnesses of flesh. For her lover she is Goya's naked Maja. She is as young as she pretends to be. She is enchantment itself.

"Suppose your husband finds out," he asks as he is buttoning his shirt.

"He won't." She blows him a kiss. "People don't discover what they don't want to know."

"You say you love me." He pulls on his slacks.

"I do."

"How can you live with him and sleep with him and not let that show?"

"I love him too. My loving you has nothing to do with my loving him."

He puts on his shoes and ties his laces and says nothing.

"If I were painting a picture," she says, "I wouldn't just use red paint. I would use blue and green and purple and yellow and maybe even a little black because I love all those colors. But I would keep the red in the red jar, the blue in the blue jar, the yellow in the yellow jar, and I would keep their respective lids on top so as not to mix them up."

"Bitch," he says, not without affection.

She laughs and, paraphrasing Edna Millay, recites: "You are but summer to my heart and not the full four seasons of the year...."

I catch her laugh between my teeth—an impossible feat, were I not smiling. I am tempted to chew up her laugh, to spit it out. Instead I remain stoically smiling. What can I say about myself that would explain?

Should I use the excuse of the holes in my head? Should I say that hunger inhabits my skull? Should I say I was shaped out of potter's clay on a day the potter was drunk? Should I tell of the consciousness that preceded my existence in the ancient kiln where I was nothing more than a shape among other shapes? Should I tell how, as he made us, even the potter didn't know how we would turn out; how some of the pieces he expected to be wonderful emerged stillborn from the fire while others he had little hope for emerged

marvelously alive? Should I tell how, when the temperature in the kiln reached its height, a magical blue-green mist shimmered around us and how this was the moment when one or another of us was touched with life? And how the potter, peering in at us at this moment, burned his eyebrows, his eyelashes and all the hair off the front of his head?

Her husband owns an oil well in Texas. He flies there from the East several times a month. So he says. She never questions these trips although he also says that younger women are "easier on the eyes" than older women.

"How fortunate," she answers to such comments, "that I intend to remain young my entire life."

He expressed this preference for younger women when they first met. She told him she was twenty although she was already twenty-five, and he still thinks she is five years younger than she actually is. She played his child bride. When she wanted to see if her two years of school French would be sufficient to order a complete meal, they flew to Paris for breakfast. They flew back to New York in time for dinner at Elaine's. During the gas crisis he hired a horse-drawn carriage to take her to the theater and home again. On their fifth anniversary he threw a party that (for its extravagance) was written up in *New York* magazine.

He filled her world with glamorous games and for eight years she was faithful to him. Then, although she continued to love him, a desolating sense of loss would periodically sweep her. To escape it she traveled, sometimes with her husband, often enough without him. It was on a visit to Machu Pichu that she found me.

Should I say we were as naturally drawn to each other as shadow is to substance? Our covenant, conducted with repeated glances, was made in silence.

Her husband is in a querulous mood. She was not at home when he arrived; it was the cook's day off and there was nothing to eat in the house.

"That's hardly my fault," she says.

"Of course it isn't. Nothing ever is your fault. I do want you to tell me, though, because I'm anxious to know, since it isn't your fault, whose fault is it?"

"Nobody's fault." She speaks with exaggerated sweetness. "You are simply being a grouch. On another day you would just have said: Listen, sweetheart, darling, light of my life, as there is nothing for us to eat here, I suggest we go out for dinner tonight."

He paces back and forth expounding on her infuriating traits. She sits down at her dressing table and becomes inordinately occupied with brushing her hair. In a while the theme of his argument has changed from her lack of interest in his comfort to her peculiar choices in friends.

"You just want to isolate me," she says sharply.

He remarks that whatever shortcomings he might have, deafness is not among them.

"All I have to do is mention a liking for someone in order for you to find something wrong with that person."

"There usually is something off key with the people you like—which makes me wonder, of course, what attracted you to me."

"There is not a single person I've liked whom you haven't belittled in some unkind way."

"I'm certain my unkind belittlings, whatever they were, were eminently justified."

"It is not justified to refer to a human being—any human being—as The Scarecrow."

"The Scarecrow?"

"Don't pretend you don't know what I'm talking about: The Scarecrow called; The Scarecrow dropped by and left this for you; The Scarecrow said this or that or the other thing."

"Oh, you mean your admirer. Well, I can hardly be blamed for his bones being visible through his skin. Besides, I use Scarecrow as a form of endearment. I could, with equal accuracy, call him The Cadaver."

"He happens to be a good friend. And quite talented."

"The ersatz Dostoyevsky? Or is it the ersatz Harold Robbins?"

"There, you see? Nothing but contempt for him as a writer, and you've never bothered to read a word he's written."

"Does it occur to you that I may not have time to plow through the lengthy scribblings of some amateur, sincere though he may be? Does it occur to you that I have a business to run? Do you ever question how much money it takes to keep a wife with extravagant hobbies afloat, a wife who, among other eccentricities, collects costly trinkets with no other purpose than to clutter up the place?"

"That is patently unfair!"

"I agree, my dear. Most of life is unfair."

"What I collect, for your information, is art."

"Oh, art? Is that what you call this freakishly endowed troll you insist on keeping up there on the mantle? I'd swear the damn thing is staring at us. Spying on us, more likely."

"That invaluable piece of pre-Columbian pottery is not spying on us. Inanimate objects do not spy."

"I'd like to know what he finds so relentlessly funny. He's constantly grinning, have you noticed?"

"*It*, not he. It happens to be a very special drinking vessel used by the ancient Peruvians in their religious rites. It was specifically designed to exorcise the demons of infertility and impotence. A magic potion was poured into its head and drunk from its phallus. And it's my guess, that if you were it, you'd be grinning too."

If only I were not forced to be the eternal observer.... I console myself with the knowledge that there is always an element of complicity between observer and those who are being observed. It is hardly an accident that I am here where I cull her triumphs, her fears, her angers, her pleasures so that they almost become my own, so that, studying her, I discover my own imperfections in the hectic glaze of her face.

I console myself by remembering that from the beginning it was easiest to remain empty, to gather the images of other lives and let them constitute my history.

Her husband has brought her a gift. She unwraps the beribboned oblong box and withdraws a vibrator. He sits on the bed and watches her examine it. It is made of pink rubber. The shaft (which ends in the head of a bearded dwarf) undulates at different speeds depending on how it is set. Perpendicular to the shaft, and attached to its base, is a beaver. If a woman inserts the shaft with the dwarf's head into herself, the beaver nuzzles her sex.

"Quite an imaginative little toy," she says.

He suggests that she use it while he watches her. She is reluctant. She thinks she would find it disturbing if he only watched and didn't touch her. Making love is, after all, something they should do together. He assures her that he will do his part. But what does he want to watch for? What does he want to see? It's simply another form of enjoyment, he says. One has five senses, after all. Why should only one or two of them be employed in making love?

She lies on the bed and presses the dwarf's head between her legs. She moves against it and emits occasional little cries. Her eyes are closed. She imagines a robber has broken into the bedroom and that it is his hand on her, his cock prying her open.

Her husband grows hard as he watches. As soon as she is finished and lays the vibrator aside, he mounts her.

Her lover is stroking her legs. She has beautiful legs, he tells her; velvet skin, like a baby's. She raises her arms and crosses them behind her head in a sultry pose she has practiced in front of the mirror. It makes her breasts look higher and fuller. She has studied the way the light falls on her and which twist, which little arch of the back or the neck will produce the most flattering effect.

Her lover seizes her and his fingers leave white marks on her skin that at once turn red. He kisses her; he grapples with her as with the raw side of a cliff: grasping, clinging, digging himself in to escape the long, treacherous fall down.

...the images of those who worshiped me. ...the memory of being worshiped. My erect phallus, nearly as large as I am; the memory of it filling mouth after mouth, hundreds of mouths: the mouths of peasants, of nobles, angry mouths, eager mouths, frightened mouths, dry mouths, moist, trusting mouths. A strange joy, a quickening wave of power flooded me as I was able, over and over and over, to satiate their diverse hungers.

They are preparing to go to a dinner party. The host is an old friend of hers. She had lost touch with him for many years and only recently met him again. He may or may not have once been her lover. These days his sexual preference is for men—which is certainly his prerogative, she tells her husband as she applies mascara lash by lash to avoid having them clump together. What she fails to understand is his predilection for violent men. When she visited him last week he was sporting three-inch-wide strips of tape around his ribs because some transient admirer of his had seen fit to kick them in.

She finishes with the mascara and begins brushing blusher onto her cheeks with upward strokes. Intermittently she sips a green stinger (the white creme de menthe ran out an hour or so ago). Her husband, who but for donning blue jockey shorts has made no attempt to get ready, is drinking neat bourbon.

"Violence as a sexual stimulant..." he says, and pauses, leaving the sentence unfinished. She continues applying the blusher and her cheeks slowly turn a feverish pink.

"Fucking, per se, is an aggressive act, you know, whether we care to perceive it as such or not. Violence does stimulate the circulation, increase the adrenaline flow, that sort of thing."

"I can't imagine getting my bones broken as conducive to anything resembling fun."

"It's not inconsistent to theorize that it may en-

hance orgasm as well. It needn't be as extreme as a case of broken ribs, of course. It needn't even leave marks."

She puts down the blusher, selects an eyeshadow, and begins to paint her lids silver. I catch her questioning look in the mirror. She glances away as though she has not seen me.

He has found an imitation leather belt among her things. She bought it to match a certain beige dress and only wore it once, deciding that, after all, it looked as cheap as it was.

"Haven't you ever been curious..." he asks, slapping the belt against his palms.

She swallows deeply, finishing her stinger before answering that, yes, she has occasionally wondered, but not with any real curiosity; not with any desire to actually experiment.

He takes their empty glasses, leaves, and returns some minutes later with fresh drinks. He finds it rather amusing, he tells her, to discover these inhibitions of hers. She denies that she has inhibitions. And if he is that keen on trying, she says, if it means that much to him...And if, in addition, he promises to stop the instant she wants him to...

He raises his glass toward her in a toast.

She stretches herself downward on the bed, her whole body taut.

The vinyl belt cuts the air with a soft whoosh like a startled exhalation. It strikes and strikes with the steady rhythm of a heartbeat. It brings a bright blush to her naked buttocks. But the stingers have had an anesthetizing effect. The blows seem no more than light glancing slaps. For some reason she remembers a butterfly she once chased in a garden, and how she wanted to catch it, hold it in her hands, see its brilliant iridescent colors very close up. And how, though she nearly caught it several times, it always eluded her.

"Harder," she begins to urge her husband, "harder."

With each singing cut of the belt the sliced air rushes against me. It vibrates through this painted body into which I could never draw real life and from which I cannot escape.

DRAGONPRINCE

"Have you had many lovers?" the Dragon asked in a casual tone the Princess soon came to recognize as a warning. He was stretched out in front of his cave, absentmindedly singeing the grass around some ants. As they scuttled away, he singed the grass in their wake. The Princess would have asked him to stop had she noticed. At the moment she was too busy massaging the iridescent green hide of his back. It gave her pleasure to do this because she knew he liked it.

"None like you," she said. "None as strong and brave."

The Dragon had made a flamboyant display of his courage at their first meeting, diving several hundred treacherous feet into a ravine to retrieve the Princess's golden apple. She had been heartbroken when it fell down there; had in fact briefly considered flinging herself after it. What she did instead was to collapse sobbing at the edge of the ravine. And then the Dragon appeared.

He offered to get the apple for her if she would make love with him afterwards. Naturally she was taken aback. It was outrageous. And from a dragon on top of everything. But, recovering from her outrage, she thought: Why not? After all, being desired is a compliment regardless of the circumstances. In addition, he can't be any worse than some of the noblemen I've had. And besides, he may not really be a dragon. For all I know, he's an enchanted prince.

To her delight the Dragon had turned out to have a pretty accomplished erotic technique. She particularly enjoyed certain effects he could produce with his fiery breath, making it ripple up and down her body like small electric singing waves.

"You are evading my question," the Dragon said.

She smiled at him. How well he knew her. It was almost as though he could read her heart. "I'm sorry," she said. "I just don't see how the others can matter now."

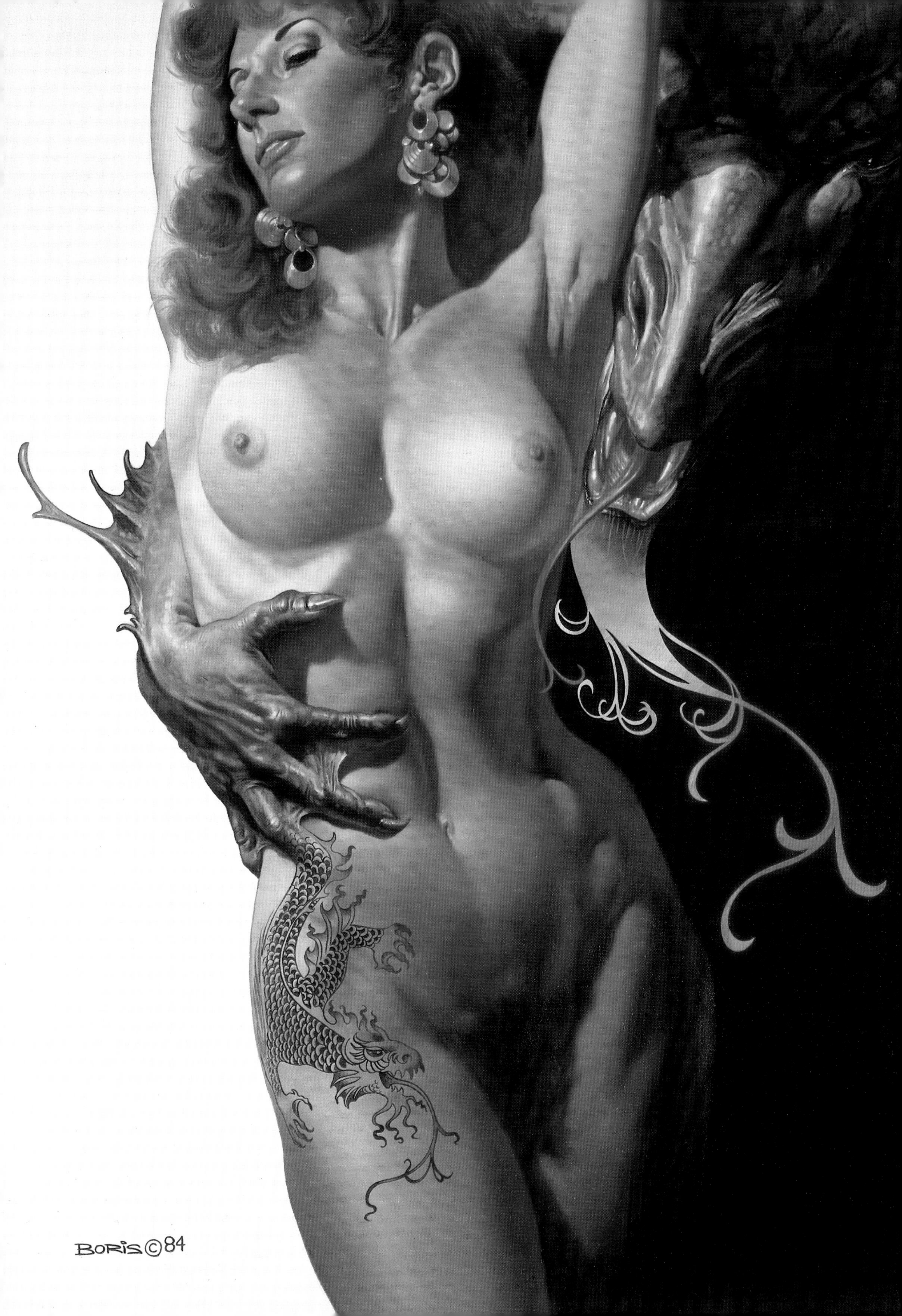
BORIS©84

"Because I want to know all about you," was the answer. "It excites me to hear about the others; appeals to the voyeur in me, I suppose. And . . ." Here he paused, as if gathering the necessary strength to continue. "I suppose that, having a dragon's typical insecurities, I want to know how I measure up against real men."

"Well . . ." the Princess began uneasily, not too happy about complying with his request but nevertheless saying to herself: Oh, what the hell, how can it hurt? "There was Rolando, who I was immensely attracted to though we had nothing at all in common. Can you imagine, he once said to me: What's the point of looking at the stars when they are so far away and there's plenty to look at right here on Earth."

"Obviously a man infatuated with mediocrity," the Dragon said.

"He was a palace guard," the Princess continued, "and married to boot. So the relationship had its limitations built in right from the start. Not only did we always have to meet when he wanted to and never when I did, but there was the guilt. Always the guilt. As if his infidelity was somehow my fault."

"An emotional cripple," the Dragon said, dismissing Rolando in half a sentence. "Was he the only one?"

"There was Justini. He not only found it interesting to look at the stars, he could name them and the constellations they were in and where they could be found in the sky and so on. But he would think nothing of making love and getting up as soon as he was finished to study his astronomical charts."

"Any more?" the Dragon ingenuously asked with no hint that, when it suited him, he would use these stories against her, would call her a pushover, a worthless cunt, and a whore in heat.

"Yes, of course there were others; always the wrong ones," the Princess said. "I wanted so very much to be loved. For years I dreamed of the prince who would come to me from somewhere far away. I used to talk about him, about what he would look like and be like. I used to have imaginary conversations with him."

"You are beautiful," the Dragon said. He rolled on his side and drew her to him. "You are beautiful," he repeated huskily, pinning her against the grass with his powerful forepaws. In less than two hours he would call her ordinary looking, a shade too large in the hips, and, what was worse, disgustingly pale. It was a great shame, he would coldly tell her, that she lacked green pigmentation. No doubt this was because she had spent so much time above ground as opposed to the revitalizing darkness of caves.

Framed against a magnificent sweep of tree-covered hills and blue sky, his great bulk seemed small and vulnerable.

"You are beautiful too," she breathed, quite meaning it.

"Don't ever leave me," he murmured.

And so they dreamed each other. Their dreams were enchanted. They became marvelous miraculous creatures, part bird, part fish, part human. They could fly clear to the sky. They could flash, silver finned, through the deepest oceans. They could promise each other eternal love.

"Yours is a classic case of insufficient parental affection," the Dragon said. "Am I right or am I right?" They had gone for a swim in the lagoon near his cave and were sunning themselves on a rock.

The Princess thought this over carefully. "They did love me. They do love me. I never doubted it in my head, you know. The difficulty has been, at times, believing it in my heart."

"The head and the heart are connected," the Dragon said, "however abstruse that connection may seem."

"My father believes in God, the power of wealth, and the inferiority of women. It doesn't make him an easy man to get close to, at least not for me."

The Dragon agreed that the King had distinct shortcomings as a father although he will later call the Princess goddamn manipulative with her wimpy ways and will, moreover, express the opinion that the King kept her at arm's length out of an admirably developed sense of self-preservation.

"My problems with the Queen were of an entirely different sort," the Princess said. "To begin with, she's a witch."

"You mean the kind that rides broomsticks?" The Dragon's green ears suddenly became very pointy.

"She wouldn't be caught dead on a broomstick," the Princess laughed. "But you should see the assortment of frog toes and lizard eyes and other motley goodies she has for mixing magic potions."

"There's nothing motley about lizard eyes," the Dragon observed dryly.

"Oh, she can do wonderful things with them," the Princess said quickly. "I've seen her throw pieces of broken glass into her cauldron and take out real diamonds."

"Can she tell the future?" the Dragon wanted to know. Upon hearing that she could, he sighed wistfully.

"Often enough I've wished that she couldn't," the Princess said. "For one thing, she's maddeningly conceited about it. And, for another, kindness and tact are not her strong points. She positively delights in grim futures. Or else she tells the future in riddles so you don't know any more when she's finished than you did at the start."

"If you're too dull to unravel riddles, that is." The Dragon's long red tongue suddenly unfurled to trap a scarlet and blue butterfly in midflight. In an instant the butterfly had disappeared into his mouth. The Princess pretended not to have seen. Whether he'd done it to shock her or because, imprisoned within a dragon's body, he had no choice, she was not sure. It seemed best, therefore, to look the other way.

"I once asked her what the prince of my dreams would look like, and this was her idea of a clever answer." The Princess sat up very straight to display the monster that had been tattooed on her midriff. "It didn't tickle in the least when she did it, I can tell you."

The Dragon was quite taken with the colorful tattoo, which, despite the intimacy of their relationship, he had not noticed before. He praised the artwork and decided, after studying it a bit, that it bore a certain resemblance to him. "A remarkable woman, your mother," he said. "I want to meet her."

This proposal made the Princess decidedly apprehensive. Though her parents professed a sufficiency of liberal ideas (And why shouldn't they? In the past witches had been burned at the stake whereas now they were being courted and fussed about to an almost imbecilic degree), in practice their code of dos and don'ts was disappointingly conservative. She could well imagine their reaction to her bringing along a dragon as a dinner guest. "Well..." she hedged, "I know my parents are both quite busy these next few weeks and—"

"What is it?" the Dragon said. "Don't tell me I'm good enough for a roll in the grass but not as an escort to the ball."

The Princess assured him that this was not, most

certainly not, the case. But secretly she berated herself. I'm the one who is really a dragon, she thought, for putting a nice face on what is, in truth, hypocrisy.

The Dragon, sensing his advantage, pressed his case in a pained, brave voice. He understood how she might find it awkward to be seen with him. She needn't explain. They were not, after all, your conventional couple. He just thought being as close as they were and understanding each other as well as they did would have neutralized, to some extent, their external differences. So it turned out that he was wrong. He didn't blame her for that; for his error in judgment. He was only sorry because such a meeting might have changed so many things for the better.

"I'm truly a beast," the Princess said.

"You are a beauty," the Dragon announced magnanimously.

"You are dear and funny and wise."

"I had only hoped that the Queen, having the talents she has..." Here he paused to lend the following words drama. "You see, I wasn't always a dragon. I was born a prince. An evil witch cast a spell on me changing me into this shape when I was quite young. I have tried not to become bitter. It is, after all, one of the things that can happen in life. But growing up as a dragon, growing up friendless, distrusted, everyone always expecting the worst from you, is difficult. Since you are an only child and know about loneliness, perhaps you can appreciate this to some degree. Children are cruel, as you may know, and I can tell you, contrary to the old saying, sticks and stones didn't come near breaking my bones but the names I was called did hurt me.

"I developed a fear of people. And I spent more and more time in my cave, sneaking out only when

I was sure no one was around. I used to dream of the time when I would have my revenge by turning into a prince and becoming the envy of all those who hated me."

"I'm just afraid for you, that's all," the Princess said. "I wouldn't want some boor to make upsetting remarks."

"I'm not afraid." The Dragon saw imminent victory.

"You're so much stronger than I am."

"It's not a matter of strength but the triumph of hope. You see, I do have great hope that the Queen will break the spell that keeps me a dragon. We could be so happy together then."

Moved by this speech, which coincided with her own dearest hopes, the Princess ignored her misgivings and arranged for the Dragon to come to dinner at the palace. The evening was a disaster.

It started in an acceptably civilized fashion with cocktails and polite if strained conversation. The Dragon was eager to ingratiate himself. He was also nervous. He drank four martinis in succession. The olives made him burp and greenish-gray smoke shot from his nostrils each time. He chattered incessantly and with increasing tempo on a variety of subjects calculated to fascinate his hosts: the decrease in swampland during the dry season and the concomitant decrease in the edible insect population; the longevity of dragons (six hundred years) and how this might well be attributed to the six-year incubation period of the dragon embryo.

When he began to suspect he was losing their attention, he switched to a repertoire of lewd jokes and then to an embarrassingly inept series of animal imitations. Clearly he had no tolerance for the combination of martinis and the wine he guzzled with his oysters on the half shell. For his bird of paradise imitation he spread his front legs out wide (to represent the bird spreading its wings) and knocked over the huge crystal wine decanter. The wine splashed all over the white tablecloth as well as on the Princess's new satin gown. Generally prepared for catastrophes of all sorts, she simply began to blot it with a napkin. He, however, leaped wildly from his chair, causing it to fall over backwards with a resounding crash. The echo of that crash seemed to go on forever.

The Queen took her daughter aside and asked her what the devil she wanted with such a weirdo.

"You've seen him at his worst," the Princess said. "It's unfair to judge him by that. He can really be very charming. Besides, he loves me."

"In my book he's a creep," the Queen replied.

The King, who basically had not expected too much, was nevertheless puzzled by his daughter's choice in a swain. "Where in the world did you unearth him?" he wanted to know. Upon hearing the story of the golden apple, how the Dragon had risked his life, the condition he'd posed but how he really loved her, he said: "To be honest with you, I don't much care for having a dragon as a son-in-law. So in case you happen to be thinking in that direction, you can do an about face. On the other hand, I'll grant you that an agreement is an agreement and, if you made it, you have to stick to it. I'm behind you all the way on that."

There it was: approval and disapproval all rolled up into one. Even if she lived as long as dragons did she would never be unequivocally in the right. But there was another thing that rankled: the Dragon's inveterate nastiness. After their brief periods of intimacy and happiness, he actually seemed to flee into rancor.

Of course, she realized, this was all due to his insecurity. Who, having once been a prince, wouldn't become insecure at one day finding himself to be a dragon? It was only natural. It was, perhaps, also natural that he was jealous of her past lovers. But his relentless carping on the subject, his disparaging criticisms were hard to take. He berated her for not having scaly skin and being unable to belch flames; for not managing to breathe under water or see in the dark; for being too cowardly to have fetched her own apple out of the ravine; too sexually inhibited to enjoy his fiery breath when it got really hot.

She recognized all this as simply being an unfortunate expression of his love for her. Yet it burdened her heavily in the long run. She knew it would probably go on for years. Still, she could hardly expect to save him, hardly expect to help him change back into a prince if she did not persevere. And there were good periods. The Dragon composed lovely poetry for her. She was his muse, he told her. This is what he recited by way of apology one afternoon when they hadn't been speaking since morning:

> I awake;
> my eyes full of dreaming
> brim with tears
> to find you real.
>
> Emptiness
> that steered my
> heart across
> deserts
> to you
> has faded like time
> into the sand.

"If your love can't turn me back into a prince, no one's can," he said when he finished.

Loving him was like plunging into the deep, deep sea at the bottom of which a treasure might lie. Loving him was quenching a lifelong thirst. Oh, she loved him from the molten core of herself clear out to her fingertips. He was all she had ever lost and stood to find again.

"If I lose you I will lose my mind," he cried to her in a voice like summer rain, full of the promises of jeweled rainbows.

Yet joy is fragile, a delicate silver shadow, shattered as readily as fine glass.

He had singed off all her pubic hair with his breath (quite deliberately, she suspected) so that her sex was suddenly bare and smooth as a peach. "Kinkily provocative-looking," he observed before he realized how angry she was about it. Subsequently he denied having anything to do with the "accident," which he came to blame on her own dragon tattoo. This was the age of magic and miracles, wasn't it? Well, the tattoo had miraculously, if only for an instant, come to life. He had distinctly seen it happen out of the corner of his eye.

At first she didn't believe he was serious. When she saw that he was, she asked tenderly if he was feeling all right. He actually snapped at her with his great gaping mouth. After that she half expected him to start foaming at the mouth, to suffer a convulsion, to fall down and beat his head against the ground or present some other evidence of having gone fatally mad. But he spoke coolly and disdainfully. He knew what he had seen. Her own dragon had caused the damage. If she chose not to believe him, that was her affair. He refused to shoulder the responsibility for her shortcomings—her paranoia, her lack of good faith, her ill humor, and so on. He scowled. He spoke through a tight, barely

moving mouth. His thick iridescent tail, which she so admired thumped the ground with impatience.

She turned and ran into the woods. The trees and hanging vines flew past her like phantoms, like mist, not quite real. In a delirium she ran from him, cursing him, calling him crazy, calling herself crazy to have stayed with him as long as she had. She might have raced on clear to the palace except that she ran out of breath. When she slowed down, the trees, the vines, the path she followed became solid and real again. She smelled smoke and came to a full stop. Let him burn himself to a crisp. Let him burn the whole forest down for all I care, I won't go back, she said to herself even as she turned around.

The fire he'd started wasn't particularly big. Only about half an acre of dry grass went. It just smoked badly. Even after the fire was out soot smudged the sky for hours.

"I'm doomed," he moaned when she found him. "I've destroyed the most wonderful thing in my life: your love for me. I have no right to it anymore. What do I, the most miserable creature in the universe, have to offer you, after all? A lifetime of living with an outcast? Of living as an outcast? You were right to leave. The noblest thing I ever did was to drive you away. My deepest wish is for your happiness. I am lost, wholly lost. I see that now. Not even you can save me. The best thing for you to do is go."

Naturally she stayed. They did not live happily ever after nor did they live entirely unhappily. Their pattern was one of fights, reconciliations, and periods of truce. They grew accustomed to it. Mysterious fires were spotted in the forest from time to time. The townspeople grew accustomed to that.

The Dragon remained a Dragon. His claim to have been a prince was wishful invention; his tale of the wicked witch and her spell, brazen fabrication.

MEDUSA

No one can tell how old she is: fresh complexioned, hazel eyes softly luminous, long black hair knotted into hundreds of tight braids, the lazy sensuality of a pampered pedigreed cat about her. All this can disconcertingly change within moments. Her face can suddenly be painted with a mad energy: metallic gleam of eyelids, fever-pink cheeks, white powder caking around the eyes that have narrowed to slits and faded to yellow. Vertical lines appear, running from nose to mouth, giving her skin the look of cracked porcelain.

Even in this frightening state there is something ineffably intriguing about her. A former lover of hers once compared this quality to the attraction that waves breaking against a cliff might have for someone standing high above them: the uncanny lure of death. Of course, he added quickly, it was not her negative charm alone that had so captivated him. She could be extraordinarily gracious, an effervescent conversationalist, an imaginative lover, and a generous patron (her wealth could not be overlooked).

She herself, obsessed with the preservation of her beauty, is not altogether sure how old she is. "After the first hundred years there's a tendency to lose count," she says with mock innocence. "And anything beyond a hundred is higher mathematics, which I don't get involved in." She throws back her head and laughs, her long braids snapping crisply as whips. "Besides, I always feel young and vital inside."

This is not altogether true. While there are the good days on which her optimism and enthusiasm seem boundless, there are the days when lethargy anchors her darkly, when every thought is poisoned with sinister premonitions and the world around her becomes brittle, thin, likely at any moment to crumble and disappear. Rain jabbers at the windows like an auctioneer frantically trying to raise the bids. Daylight turns lead gray. In the orchard the apple trees,

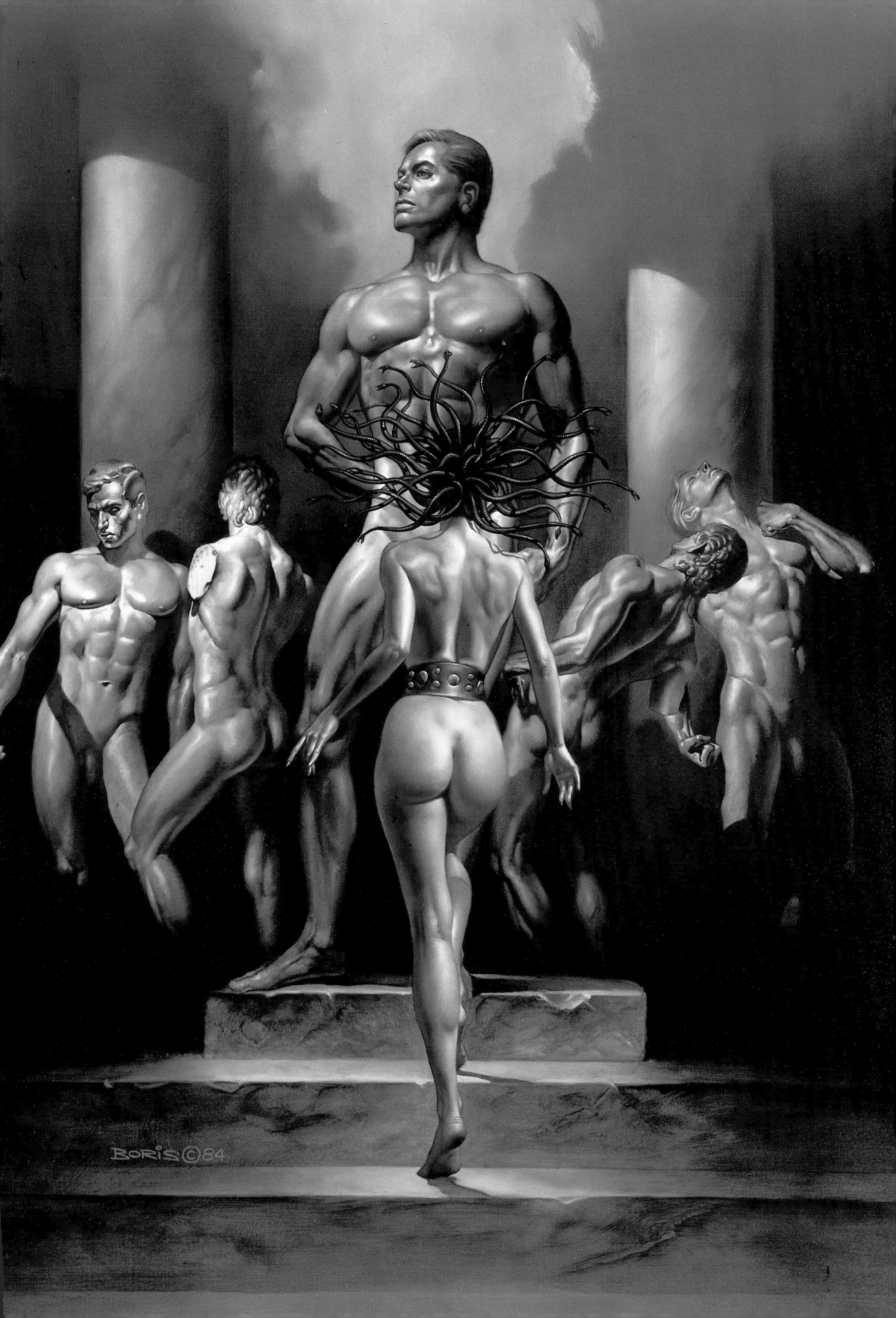
BORIS ©84

flattened against a wasted sky, appear barren, incapable of ever again producing even a single green leaf. The servants deliberately misunderstand her requests and her lovers ruthlessly bore her.

She wanders through the elegant rooms with their paintings, their tufted couches, their French windows, and stokes her smoldering grievances. Warmth defiantly seeps from the expensive house; the blue creeps from the sky. Time, that has caught her willy-nilly in its current, rushes her toward some dank, inhospitable downstream where all her magic will turn dull and dross, where the brilliance of a skyrocket will become the crack and fizzle of a cheap firecracker. She rails at the sky, the rain, the rooms, and the volitant, vanishing minutes. It is just when she is most desperate that all of nature conspires to ignore her.

What is left, then?

Who is left?

Pancho. Her lover. Traditionally handsome, broad-shouldered, narrow-hipped, with beautifully sculpted muscles beneath smooth, cool skin, he is eternally ready with a compliment. And he never fails to laugh (insincerely, perhaps, but convincingly) at her witticisms and at her cynically humorous observations.

Pancho.

He appears as soon as she calls.

Actually, his name is not Pancho. His real name is unimportant. It is even possible that he has no real name. She calls all her lovers Pancho, as much for the coarsely exotic sound of the name as for a secret hankering for the barbaric embraces of Pancho Villa, whose legend electrifies her fantasies.

Pancho!

They appear as soon as she calls. Today there are three of them. There are never less than two and often as many as five or six. This is necessary, since the real-life Pancho, restricted as he would have been by time and space, could never have been as fully ambidexterous as the ersatz Panchos. For instance, with six Panchos to make love to her, one might lick her neck and blow gentle kisses into her ears, while another played with her breasts, still another suckled engagingly at her clitoris, a fourth probed her deliciously sensitive rear, a fifth stroked and fondled her toes and the slim, high-arched soles of her feet, while the sixth photographed the group, capturing various positions from various angles (the pictures are mounted in a special leather-bound book) and functioned as prop man in a sense, bringing the thin black riding whip, the silk ropes, the ice cubes, the vibrating dildo —whatever was called for.

She never thinks of her lovers in the plural. To her they are interchangeable singulars. It is as if they appear to be more than one only through a failure of

the retina to receive a properly focused image.

They enter the bedroom already obviously aroused, eager. They are naked, hairless, smooth as polished marble. Being marble, they can exist in a perpetual state of arousal and eagerness for her. This, in any case, is their duty.

She half-sits half-reclines against the plumped-up pillows of her circular bed. Her yellow eyes are starkly outlined in purple. This gives her an eerily predatory look.

Behind her throne of pillows stands a ten-foot-tall statue, a naked male sculpted out of white Carrara marble. At first glance he is truly awesome. The skill of the unknown sculptor was such that the statue appears alive. The veins beneath his glowing skin seem flushed with blood. He seems to breathe. Clearly, his magnificent chest expands and contracts with breath. The warmth emanating from his body, his sensual odor, the white pearl of cum tantalizingly visible at the tip of his gleaming-hard phallus—he too is Pancho.

Once the mind has suggested that he might be alive, he is (except for the difference in size) identical with the other Panchos.

It is possible that she has been drinking. She frequently drinks to counteract the intrepid flow of life toward a bleak horizon. Drinking imbues her with preternatural powers. She shakes her head and the long braids, hissing sharply, coil and uncoil like snakes.

The Panchos freeze, becoming white as the giant statue. Perhaps, indeed, they turn to statues. Her glance shatters against them and falls tinkling to the floor. Interpreting their unresponsiveness as insolence, she flings a half-empty bottle of gin at them.

Pancho: the dampening in his armpits.

Pancho: the acceleration of his pulse.

Pancho: the tensing of his body against the impact.

The bottle strikes the most vulnerable part, the erect phallus. It breaks off with a crack and drops like a stone. The expectant expression he had on his face when he entered the bedroom does not change. The gin bottle shatters into jewel-bright tears.

He is, even as an amputee, still quite handsome. The sight of his emasculated figure disturbs her, however, and she goes in search of a tube of glue, which she discovers in a drawer between stockings and panties.

She applies the glue both to the broken end of the phallus and the junction between pelvic region and thighs where it belongs. She is somewhat piqued. These things shouldn't be so fragile, she thinks. They shouldn't break apart at the least excuse. Look at me. Look at all I have to deal with. And I can't afford to break apart.

Gradually, as the phallus she holds to the sticking place warms in her hand, she is mollified. The con-

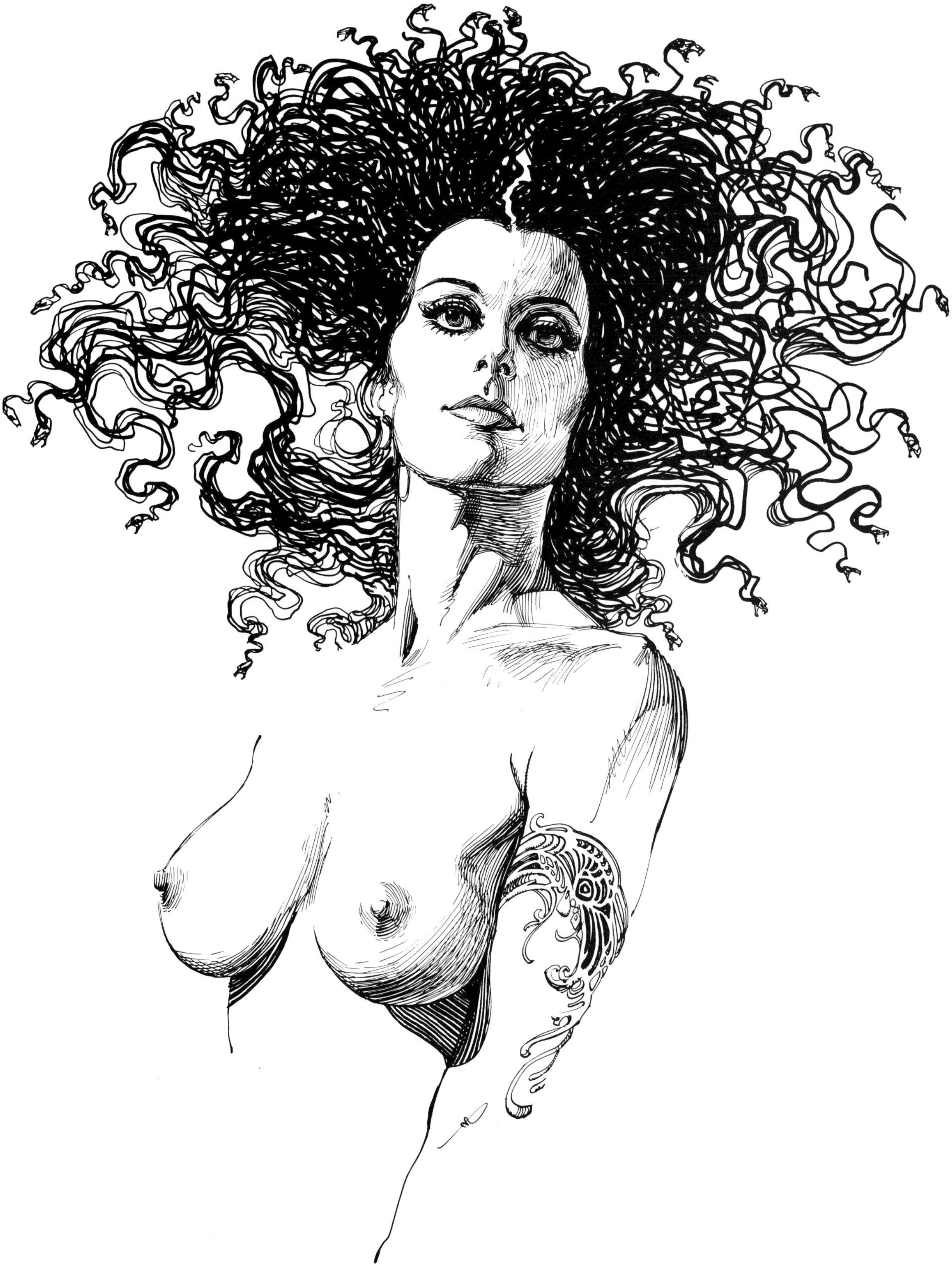

venient thing about Pancho's phallus is that, regardless of the circumstances, it is always reliably hard. "Shall we test you now," she says. "Shall we see how good I am at putting this dear Humpty Dumpty together again?"

The convenient thing about Pancho is that he can always be put together again. If she knocks off an ear, a nose, an arm—which, with her roller-coastering temper, is inevitable—it can be glued back without difficulty.

She kneels, runs her thumb and forefinger from the tip to the base of the phallus and back again. "I dreamed that this was a great big candy cane you had between your legs," she says. "And that I rolled it between my fingers until the sugar melted into sweet, flowing sap."

Pancho confirms that it is a candy cane.

She sucks at it thirstily as if to drain all its sap at once. There is something animallike in her zeal, her rapacity. One almost believes she will suck him dry, leaving only the husk. Of course this is impossible. To assume that Pancho is made of marble is to assume he cannot be sucked dry.

Even Pancho would confirm this. It would be confirmed, also, by the subsequent games she plays with him, which, were he no more than a husk, he would crumble under. When he lies flat, his phallus perpendicular to the ground, she crouches above him. She plays piston to his piston rod. They go fifty, eighty, a hundred miles an hour, taking leaps, drops, incredible swerves, finally breaking the sound barrier before they roar through the finish line and, drenched, breathless, exhausted, gradually return to zero again.

When he kneels behind her she also kneels, the globes of her buttocks spread, and the tossing, pitching race begins anew. Pancho can be behind her, in front of her, above her, beneath her simultaneously.

Although racing quickens her pulse and respiration and is the usual antidote for lethargy, it does not always help. Today, for instance, she finds Pancho, on the whole, rather irritating. He is too predictable, too acquiescent, too mundane. All his ideas are pale renditions of her own. His most appealing poses and gestures strike her as mimicry. All innovations he brings to their lovemaking have been gotten out of a *How to...* book. He has been indiscreet enough to leave it lying in plain sight.

She glances through it, recognizing, among the illustrations, his latest moves. Thus provoked, she throws it at him. It strikes him full in the face, and the force with which it was flung breaks his neck. His head falls to the ground and rolls a little way like a ball. One more thing for her to fix. At the moment she is hardly in the right frame of mind for fixing.

The sheepish Pancho stands, headless, between the bed and the door. She flounces past him, resisting the impulse to give the head a good kick. The possibility of a fractured skull (which would mean still more repairs) cannot be discounted. As it is, all repairs must wait for later, when she feels less agitated.

She wraps herself in a long fur-trimmed cloak and goes outside. It is much warmer than she had expected. The sun, which had been lulling half asleep in the sky, catches fire just as she emerges from the house. The rain has stopped, and the pitiless winter backdrop has been replaced by a fresh and green spring setting.

Perhaps all the trouble was simply a matter of breathing stale air for too long, breathing the tired odor of statues that were, after all, not truly alive. Then this outing was the answer. She would come back heartened, revitalized. She hopes Pancho will have the good sense not to be hanging around the bedroom when she returns, his head still on the floor in the corner.

The lawns are a rich green velvet through which a trim flagstone path has been laid. It leads past brilliant blooming flowerbeds, fountains, perfectly pruned fruit trees, and across a small bridge that spans a softly trilling stream. The path ends at a charming shaded grotto. Here the stream becomes a miniature fall, a cascade of silvery sparkling banners unfurling into a deep blue natural basin.

Seated on one of the flat stones bordering the basin, his chin supported by one hand, his elbow in turn resting on his knees, and seemingly contemplating the intense almost unnatural blue of the water pooling at his feet, is the statue of a superb young man.

She looks at him with a bemused expression on her face; his golden hair, his tan body. She does not remember ordering a statue for the grotto, although the idea has occurred to her in the past. This grotto, notched into the hillside and hidden from the rest of the estate by a wall of flowering rhododendron, a paradisial and very private setting, is the ideal place for making love.

When, distracted by her unexpected appearance, he raises his head, she is struck by the incredible blue of his eyes. As blue as the deepest blue of the water. She thinks, absently, that it is a remarkable color for marble. "Pancho...?" she says tentatively.

She is mistaken, he tells her or seems to tell her. He is not Pancho. His name is... The sound flows past her musically without coalescing into an actual name. For her he is Pancho. The wonderful play of his muscles as he moves, straightens, rises... The controlled strength of his body... He is unbelievably graceful, unbelievably sensual. The sight of his bare torso alone is enough to set her keening with heat.

Pancho.

She smiles at him, invites him with her smile. She opens her arms to receive him. She is radiant with anticipation.

He looks at her without recognition. As if she is a stranger. As if he doesn't understand what she wants. In reality this improbable behavior must just be part of a new theme he is introducing, a new twist to the game of lover and beloved.

"Pancho," she murmurs, "how splendid to find you here."

He seems to answer, and she nods as if in agreement. Whatever his answer is can't possibly matter. She is not in the habit of listening to his words for their meaning, only for their soothing melody.

Since he chooses, this time, to play the beloved, she will play the lover. Confident in this role, she approaches him. Without moving, however, without even taking a breath, he is strangely elusive. It is as if her hands gliding across his chest, his hips, his buttocks, leave no impression, do not even touch him. His cool, polished flesh remains indifferent. His phallus, rocked and cradled in her hands, is a sleeping kitten, soft and helpless. She bends and kisses it. She licks it like a mother cat, prods it to waken, but it slumbers, unheeding.

The danger, she realizes all at once, the very real danger is that he may be laughing at her behind the opaque blue eyes, the insensate armor of flesh. Crouched inside the impudently sleeping phallus he may be laughing contemptuously; critical of her face, her body, her words, of all the gestures she makes in desiring to be desired.

She looks at him and sees her worst suspicions mirrored in his eyes: her own face—distorted in the twin arcs of his corneas—gleaming with fury.

Certainly, what has happened is that she had been too generous, too permissive, letting him wander out here—in the singular—where he has no business, letting him initiate the rules of the scene. "Don't think I don't know what you're trying to do," she hisses. What has happened is that she has been too agreeable. That can change, as he should all too well know. How presumptuous of him to think otherwise.

In an instant she has picked up a rock and struck him on the temple with it.

But now a totally unexpected phenomenon takes place. The marble face tears open where it has been struck. A wound shows, raw as a maddened eye, a wound that will not be complaisantly healed up with glue. How is this possible? Blood streams over the blanching curve of his cheek, rivulets of red tears.

She steps back, away from him, incredulous. Could she have caused such damage? Perhaps, she thinks, this might be yet another trick. "Ingrate," she cries, more in panic than anger. And then, with the first chill stab of a grotesquely odd idea, she adds, "Who are you?"

He gives her a name with which she is wholly unfamiliar.

SHOWTIME

I am nothing
   but my long road,
   my gains and losses,
   words and silences,
   refusals and coerced agreements.

A dancing marionette
   collapsed between acts,
A stumbler
   seeking answers with a white-tipped cane,
A drowner
   struggling in a dry sea,
An insomniac
   scratching the dust for dreams.

Will you love me
   for my yeses
   though they are make-believe?
Need me
   for pretending
   there are no nos?

   I'm sure that anyone reading this poem of mine will notice startling inconsistencies between it and the way they see me. To some extent this is only natural, because I am always changing. One minute I'm laughing, the next minute I'm sad. Which is not to imply that I am schizophrenic, merely hypersensitive to my surroundings. A withered leaf fluttering on a bare branch might move me to tears.

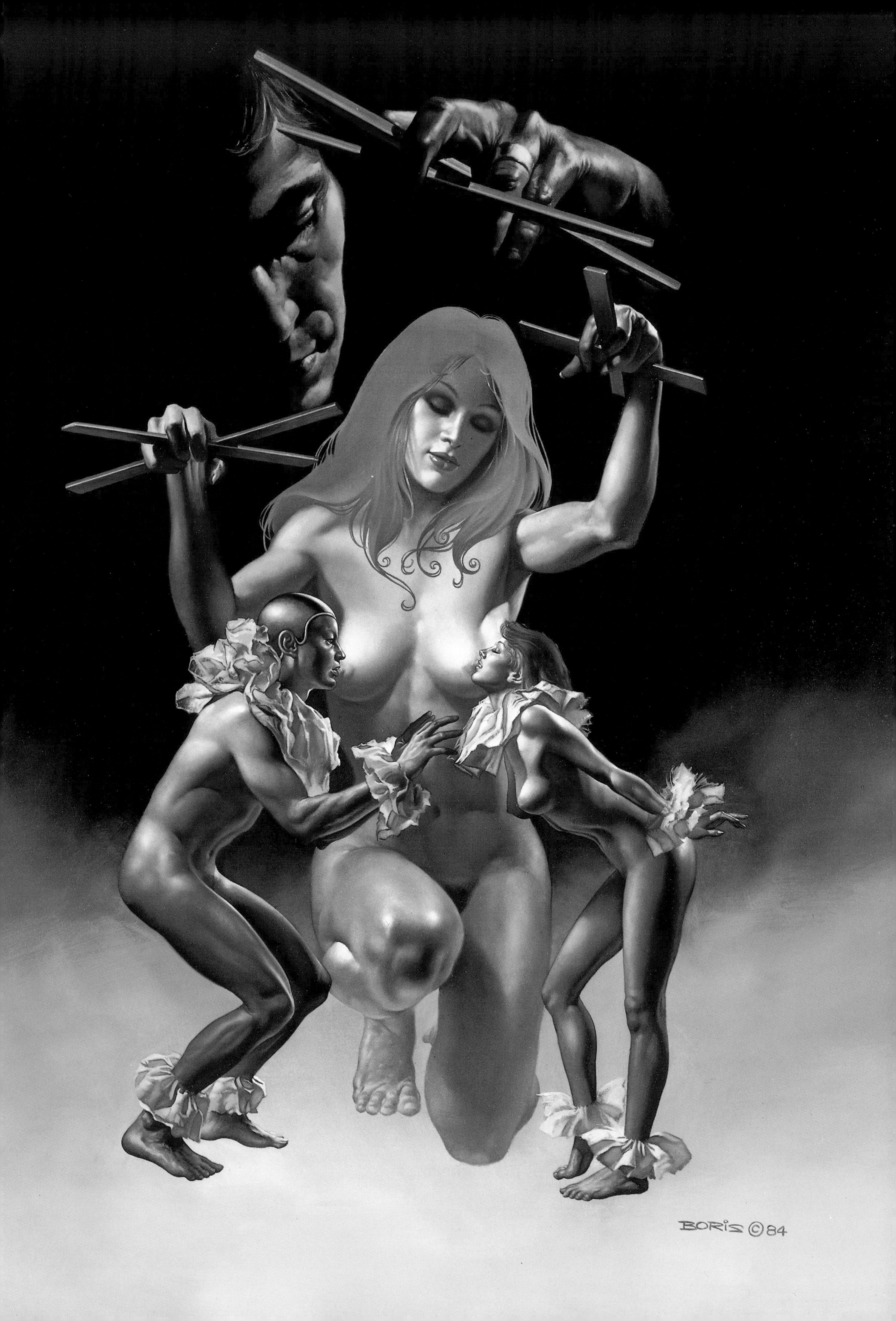
BORIS ©84

Sometimes I think I should write everything down just as I experience it; everything that happens, everything that is said. I should catch it before it changes, preserve it like the imagery fixed in a poem. I do think of my life as a kind of poem, a unique succession of contrasting pictures.

The problem with trying to capture these pictures (as if they were leaves forever pinned to their branches) is the problem of truth, the danger of quite innocently choosing the wrong word or phrase and thereby painting a wholly fallacious scene.

Take the phrase: *A dancing marionette/ collapsed between acts.* What do you think of? A painted face, a frozen smile, a wooden torso and limbs connected by metal joints; a helpless thing, all its movements determined by whoever manipulates its strings. Well, to some extent that is true enough. And, conversely, it is revoltingly false. If I were incapable of raising my own arms or of kicking up my own heels, I would not be writing poems, obviously.

Furthermore, that unfortunate phrase connotes some vexation with having one's leaps and landings, pirouettes and curtsies determined by the pluck and pull of strings. In fact, just the reverse is true. To have all one's flights and tumbles taken care of, one's smallest gestures directed (so to speak) from above, is an extraordinarily soothing experience—quite like having a good massage. One doesn't have to fear, to hesitate, to wish, to wonder what the next, best step would be. One can dance and fall asleep and keep right on dancing. I sleep with my eyes open. I can do this without any difficulty at all.

To have called myself an insomniac on this account was just taking poetic license. The fact is, I have no trouble sleeping at all. If anything, I have trouble staying awake. Or (often enough) determining whether I am really awake or asleep, whether what passes in front of my eyes is real or not. Sometimes it is impossible to tell the difference between what I am actually doing and what I seem to be doing, what I truly feel and what I seem to feel.

It may happen, between the acts, that my head, dropping suddenly to my chest, jerks me awake. And thrown so abruptly off balance, I realize with a kind of queasy disappointment that I have not been awake all along. I have not been dancing or laughing or making love. I have not been taking bows. I have not been hearing applause. I have been asleep. During the performance, on the other hand, I am safe from these awakenings. I can't possibly lose my balance, because he is in charge of it.

He has a light, inspired touch, quite like a musician's. When he plays my strings, sleep flows into wakefulness and back to sleep as smoothly as sand through an hourglass. Does this explain how a seemingly constricting experience might be satisfying? lulling? addictive, even?

Clearly, it is a tricky business to avoid propounding half-truths and misconceptions in one's poetry. Even if all one wants to write about is the simplest of matters —the scene outside this window, let's say. A seemingly uncompromising beginning might go as follows: *The sun is shining. The sky is clear. The yellow curtains in the window of the brownstone across the street look freshly laundered and starched. The stoops have been swept.* All this would strike you as very golden and warm. But it happens to be twenty degrees below zero outside on that street, which, at the moment, is empty. Should anyone come by, hands thickly gloved, head partly retracted into the sheltering collar of a down vest, his breath would form icicles at the end of his nose; icicles that might well break off and bounce on the sidewalk like marbles.

Or, let's say, one begins on a slightly different note. The emphasis is on time, not on temperature. One might start writing again about the sun, which is shining; the sky, which is clear. The reader naturally believes it is a beautiful morning, that a day rife with possibilities is beginning. And then, by some word or sound (perhaps the chance ringing of a church bell somewhere in the distance), the appalling discovery is made that it is not morning at all. It is four in the afternoon. The morning has vanished unremarked and it is already too late to do any of the things that might once have been possible.

I will have to tear up the poem I wrote earlier (I say "earlier" instead of "this morning" since mornings do blend so treacherously with afternoons that there is no way of being certain what time a particular event occurred) because, rereading it, I was disturbed by its complaining tone, its cynicism, which was not what I intended. I had certainly not intended to give so grim an impression of my relationship with him.

There are people who, with a few words, can create precise and vivid imagery. Unfortunately, I am not one of them. If he were lost and it were up to me to give the police a description of him, they would never find him. Sometimes he is a giant. His hands, fingertips to wrists, as long as my own self, head to toe. At these times I can hardly make out his face, which sways somewhere above me like a great formless cloud. And his voice, disembodied, patters around me like a warm rain. Naturally I have difficulty understanding what he tells me at these times.

"What is it that you love about me?" I once asked him during such a time. I did feel loved, but markedly

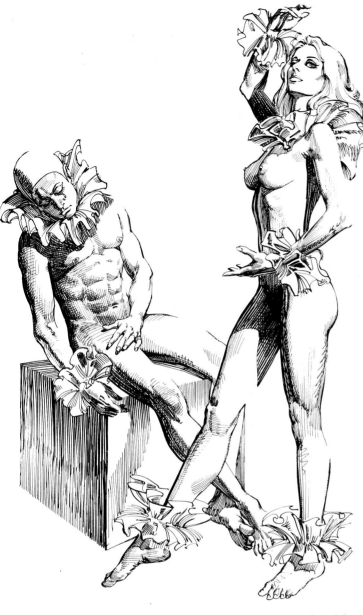

uneasy as well. As if I could lose whatever lovable qualities I had unless he pinpointed them exactly. The sound of his answer, though temporarily sustaining, left me no wiser.

He can also be incredibly small, so fragile and frightened, so seemingly lost as to seem like someone else entirely. I feel terribly sad for him then. Terribly loving. I do want to comfort him, to rock him in my arms. But there is the bewildering possibility of crushing him to contend with. He appears so shockingly delicate. His skin is translucent. I'm afraid touching him, even lightly, would cause him to bleed.

"I am a terrible poet," I commented yesterday or possibly last week.

"So what," he said. "You don't have to be a poet."

He makes no attempt to appreciate my struggle. He sees no purpose in writing poetry, in weighing and balancing words, in holding them up to the light to see their colors change, in striking them, like a tuning fork, against the soul.

His hobby is photography. "A photograph," he says, "is more accurate than words and less alterable than memory."

He keeps a large manila envelope filled with photographs of me in the middle drawer of his desk. I have not looked at them for a while. As long as I can, I resist the temptation (nearly always present) of looking at them. Not that he would care in the least if I rummaged through his pictures of me and tossed them out all over the room or flung them up in the air in handfuls and let them snow down all around; all the right and left profile shots, the full-face shots, the shot of me peeking coquettishly over my shoulder and wearing only a scarlet feather boa.

I am afraid to look at them too often lest they lose their effectiveness. I save them for emergencies. For when the pain or—more specifically—the sense of non-being becomes too strong. I wait as long as I can bear it. And then I pounce on them. I clutch them, memorize them, devour them and, finally, for a while I am satiated. Finally I see myself as he sees me. Finally I am reassured that I am.

Of course my photographs are nothing more than two-dimensional representations of me. I understand that perfectly well. It is me that I don't understand. About anyone else I can know at a glance if they are pleased, angry, disinterested, sleepy, eager to make love. About myself, I am never completely sure. I seem to lack a heartbeat, to lack a skeleton, to lack flesh and blood. (Have I inadvertently put my finger on the trouble here? I am a marionette, after all.)

In the photographs my face smiles, frowns, projects variously wistful and seductive moods that in anyone else would be unambiguous. People say that it is an attractive face, which leads me to the conclusion that it has to be. They would not speak with such assurance if there were any doubt.

What worries me is that I apparently miss what for them is self-evident. The combination of blue eyes, blond hair, red lips, and a small upturned nose does not constitute beauty for me any more than a piece of music that may have been written but never played. Still, I don't want to sound ungrateful. I would rather be called beautiful than ugly. Just as I would rather be agreed with than criticized.

Some painters arrived here earlier. In no time an entire flat had been painted the most exquisite sky blue. As soon as it dried, I heard one of them say, they would have to paint clouds on it—white clouds, to be sure, not gray ones or thunderclouds. If they'd asked me, I would have told them to leave it the way it was. A cloudless sky is always nicer. Naturally they were

not about to ask me. I was not the one who ordered the flat painted in the first place.

Pretty soon there will be a costume fitting—a colossal waste of time and money, certainly. I am exactly the same size and shape that I have been all my life. And how much fitting can be done on feathers and fringes? He has decided on new color schemes. Everything in purples and greens now, as opposed to pinks and reds. As if it made a great difference. He threw out cartloads of pink net stockings, garter belts with exquisite tiny red roses, red satin gowns, and robes trimmed with marabou. I know he didn't do this to upset me, which is why I haven't told him that I wanted to keep these things or that I wish he'd at least have asked me before getting rid of them all. I know that I shouldn't get upset about this business. It's absurd, after all, for a marionette to grouse about costumes and color schemes.

It does occur to me that *once a marionette* need not mean *always a marionette.* It would be a relatively simple act to cut off the strings. The idea is not without appeal. Like the knowledge of a secret door, an escape hatch through which I could slip any time at all—should the need arise. At the moment there is no real need. At the moment, at least, I always know what to expect.

When he walked in (after the set painters left), I knew as soon as he opened the door that he wanted to make love. I was simultaneously flattered and aware of an acute, even painful anxiety lest I disappoint him, lest he came with inflated expectations that I could not fulfill. It shouldn't matter to me, I know. Even if I do disappoint him, nothing will change. Nothing can change. It would take great joy or great despair to change anything. I suspect we have neither, which, however unrewarding, provides security. He is there. I respond to his attention with affability, to his neglect with petulance. And so, for better or worse, I am bound to him.

He came in with Pierrot and Pierrette, their heads lolling against his shoulders, their legs dangling, their strings twisting and untwisting in the air.

He also calls them Abelard and Heloise or Punch and Judy or John and Jane, depending on his mood. Today they were Pierrot and Pierrette. I could tell by their costumes: clown hats, sequined harlequin masks, oversized ruffles around their necks, wrists, and ankles. I though it would take him a while to untangle their strings but he did it in a jiffy, leaving no time for polite conversation or other niceties.

"Showtime," he barked.

Pierrot and Pierrette jumped to attention like little soldiers. I took my time. How did he expect us to work up any passion for this if it was approached like an army drill?

We did not use the backdrop of blue sky and clouds but one made of velvet and mirrors in which the three of us were multiplied endlessly, each act an opulent teeming display. "The Daisy Chain" became an undulating bouquet, "Around the World" a universe of swarming bodies, and "Water Games" a garden filled with sprinkling statuary.

At some point I noticed Pierrette had a raffish magenta phallus in her hand and was licking the tip of it as if it were an ice cream pop. It matched the ruffles she wore.

I had been lying on my back. Pierrot had just risen from between my legs. Settling herself in his place, she strapped the phallus to her chin, where it made a strange-looking uptilted goatee. How can I take this seriously, I thought. She nuzzled me with it, her eyes smiling playfully behind her glittery mask. She edged forward, gently, slowly dipping it in and out of me, nipping and licking my most sensitive spot. Quite forgetting my cues, my predetermined sighs and poses, I arched toward her mischievous mouth that was causing such a blissful, tickling warmth to spread through me; her mouth that was consuming me, that was stopping my breath, that was making me cry out loud.

And then it was over. She sat up, unstrapped the phallus, and tossed it aside with a joking remark. Pierrot laughed good-naturedly.

Pierrot and Pierrette: they are friendly enough. They are also full of preposterous stories. I can never believe them. Pierrot told about a woman he met, a stunning woman, he claimed, with outrageously flashy clothes, silver hair, and great round breasts as big as volley balls. He was fascinated by her. He was crazily in love. For two weeks he played the idiot, going to see her nightly in the club where she sang in her deep, rough, aching voice. Her bittersweet songs went sharp as arrows to his heart. For two weeks he suffered as if from a high fever.

Then she agreed to take him home with her, where he discovered that she had a magnificent penis to complement her magnificent breasts. They spent the night together and experimented with various positions that he, as a man, had taken with other women but had not himself experienced as a more passive lover.

By morning he was cured of his infatuation. He boasted about his transformation from lover to cynic as if this were remarkable and enviable. I think he must have read the whole story (or one quite similar) in a magazine. He is in the habit of making no distinction between his fantasies and what really happens.

Pierrette is just the same. Her life, to hear her talk, is an endlessly superb adventure accompanied by trumpets, cannonfire, and adulation.

They are entertaining, the two of them. I won't deny that I enjoy their stories, which make the time pass pleasantly. I would prefer to believe them. The truth is, though, that the only real events in our lives are the shows we put on. We never leave this place. So, whatever happens outside, happens to someone else. We could leave here, of course. We are free to leave here.

It was obvious that he had enjoyed our little presentation. For some moments after we had finished, he was absolutely still. Then he reached into our midst, picked me up by the waist, and held me in his hand.

"That looked very good," he said. "You have no idea how exciting it is to see you begin to tremble, to see your nipples stiffen with pleasure. I can tell by your movements exactly what you are feeling. Did you know that as you approach your orgasm you hold your breath?"

He rubbed one finger back and forth across my nipples until they stiffened again. And then he pressed the same finger against my sex.

"Once I watched a stallion mounting a mare," he said. "The mare had been hobbled to prevent her from kicking though it was apparent, from the way she stood with her back arched and her hind legs apart, that she was eager enough to receive him. She was motionless as a statue, frozen in that position of offering herself. The stallion's member became extraordinarily distended. I was violently aroused by the sight of it; forceful, glistening, pumping tirelessly in and out. I felt as if I were also fucking the mare."

Rag-limp, I lay in the palm of his hand, listening without hearing. He stood up, holding me belly down. My arms and feet swayed high above the ground. This will hurt, I thought, suddenly afraid. I was glad he could not see my face, which must have been ugly

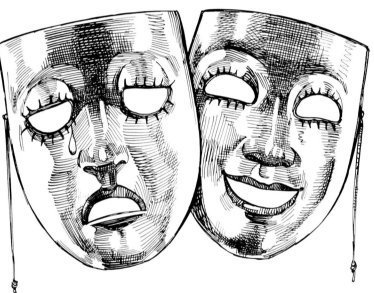

with apprehension. But he was already telling me how beautiful I was and how much he loved me. And he drilled away ruthlessly as if I were no more than a block of wood into which he was boring a hole.

Of course, since he did carve and shape me out of wood a long time ago, he would consider my objections ridiculous. If I were to tell him that I find this way he has of satisfying himself insultingly impersonal, he would laugh. I did broach it once in a mild way. I said, "I don't like the feeling, when we do it this way, that I've turned my back on you."

His answer to that was, "It feels good this way."

When he finished, he set me back down on the ground between Pierrot and Pierrette and left. It was then that I wrote the poem, which, I guess, I will tear up. I wrote it, in particular, to hurt him. Tit for tat—that sort of thing. I shouldn't stoop to such pettiness. What is the point of accusing him? He doesn't realize that there is more to me than what he once whittled out of slumbering wood. Being misunderstood is not what I object to. What hurts me is being treated as though I did not quite exist.

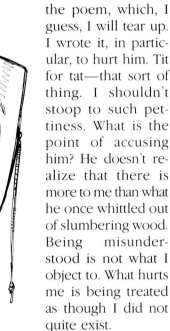

Pierrot told another one of his stories. A friend of his was living in a place that had become infested with rats.

"I'm the only person I know, " he told Pierrot, "who has to knock on my own door before I come in." One Friday he decided that he couldn't stand living like that anymore and made an appointment with a moving company to pick up his things the very next day. An hour later he was suddenly struck by the fact that he didn't have any place to move to.

I mentioned my own discontent with what goes on around here, which, I felt, was somehow paralleled in his story.

Pierrette was peculiarly unsympathetic. "One lives the way one does because one likes it," she said.

ANGEL

He sat in a room with a blanket nailed over the window. Or he walked back and forth in the room. There was a mattress on the floor, a paint-flaking wooden chair and table, a ripped bedsheet, empty beer cans, bread crusts, paper bags, wrinkled candy wrappers. Part of this mess had been kicked toward the center of the room and part toward the wall, to afford him a circular track in which to walk. From time to time he talked, gestured, propounded various arguments, quite logically. Quite sanely.

The neighbors will attest, later, to the ordinariness of his demeanor. That is, until the day it seemed something terrible must be going on in his room, a violent fight, a life-and-death battle surely, except that when the police finally broke in (they had been on the scene for close to four hours, awaiting a search-and-seizure warrant, before making their move), he was all alone. The entire ruckus, the crashing, the cursing, the screaming, was his own. He had been pounding his fists and head against the wall, obsessed with his own destruction, delirious.

No one could make sense of his rantings. He was lean, muscular, light as a boxer on his feet and as punishing as a boxer with his hands. It had taken six men to get him cuffed and trussed and bustled down three rickety flights of dark stairs, through the crowd of gawkers and squawkers that had gathered in the blistering noon sun to watch, and into the blue-and-white patrol car.

"Is that him?" a curly-haired boy asked his frowning mother.

"Is that he," she corrected.

By "he" was meant a Jack the Ripper–style executioner, the subject of much journalistic excitement over the past nine months, during which he had stabbed twelve blond women to death.

It was he. The newspapers subsequently confirmed this even as they re-

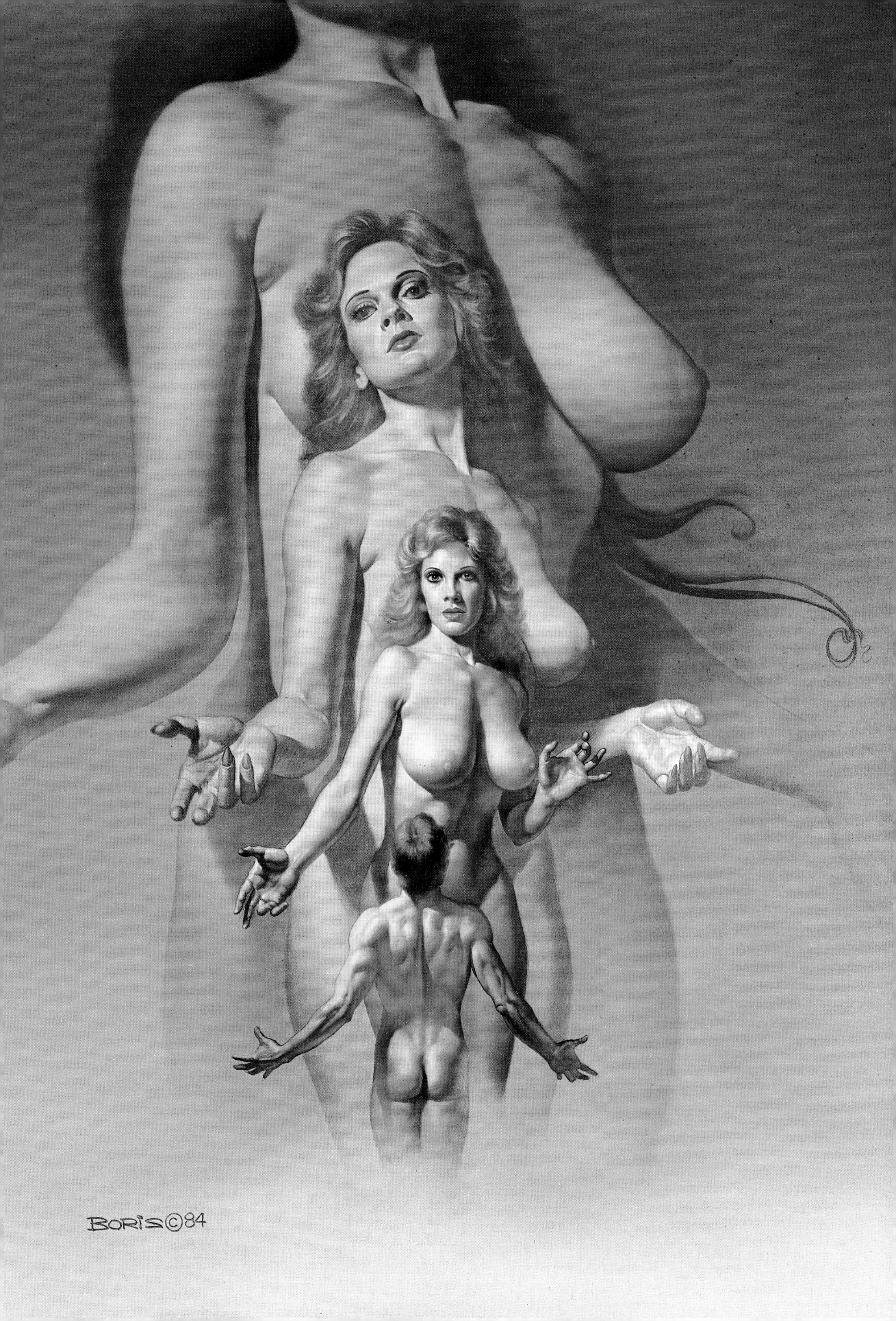
BORIS©84

marked on his docile, wholly cooperative attitude toward his interrogators; his baroque though quite serious explanation for the murders, his obvious education (he was not, contrary to the popular theories on the causes of sociopathic behavior, the product of a deprived upbringing), and, most surprisingly, his rather ingenuous sincerity.

"I would like you to know the way it was," he said. "The way it actually happened to me, step by step. But my brain, unfortunately, is a sieve. The really important things, the main events, catch there all right. The rest—the details, the chronology, the names, the places—have a tendency to leak out and get lost. But I don't want to confuse you, gentlemen. And, seeing the cynical expressions already beginning to set on your faces, it would be better, perhaps, to simplify even that which I remember. I don't want to cause any more trouble for you people than I already have."

Accordingly, the story followed of the lover he stabbed, her reincarnation, the second slaying, and the horror of all the successive reincarnations and homicides.

He sits in his cell as he once sat in his squalid room. Or, he paces back and forth. Bars have replaced the blanket as barricade across the window. He is safe, he thinks. He must be safe here. And as there is not much to do but sit or pace or think, he does a great deal of thinking although, clearly, he would be better off not to. His recollections of the recent past have such poignant immediacy. Playing and replaying his unedited nightmare, he must repeatedly suffer its torments afresh. *He must repeatedly suffer.* He will never have suffered enough, he comes to understand as his mind unwillingly reels and unreels the pictures, the words, the wrenching echoes...

The first psychiatrist to interview him will note his strong, rather handsome features: prominent cheekbones, finely chiseled mouth, straight nose, and disturbingly luminous eyes. He will write in his report that the defendant exhibits exaggerated feelings of self-importance together with an apparent inability to feel remorse. That he suffers from a narcissistic personality disorder and a frequently distorted sense of reality. The fact that he speaks of writing his memoirs, in this case, is indicative of the disorder.

I move through a world of blinding darkness. Black lightning illuminates humanity in flashes, catching it jerkily in the act of living or dying, casting familiar shadows in the dazzling night that are torn away by the dawn and scattered like rags.

But here, in this world, reality and illusion are both the same. Therefore, it is up to me to distinguish between them, to establish an order: a time for day and a time for night. Can time truly be divided in half? Half for sleep, half for waking? Does truth exist, or merely the absence of falsehood? Does love exist, or merely the absence of indifference?

I look at the woman. She looks at me. Lover and beloved. Neither of us remembers how it began. Do beginnings exist or is there merely the absence of a past? We look at each other. We have looked at each other. We will look at each other. And the answers lie beyond what we see.

"Don't we know each other?" she says.

Sometimes I say this and she remains silent.

This time she is wearing a black turtleneck jersey, a striking contrast with her long blond hair. Her breasts move softly beneath the fabric as she shifts invitingly from one stiletto-heeled foot to the other. Her smile is irresistible.

When I lie down and she bends over me, her hair spills across my mouth. I long to capture the light in her eyes; that magical sparkling like a sky full of fireflies or like tiny, tiny Chinese lanterns dancing on an invisible string. When I lie down and she grinds herself full length against me, her breasts (with their nipples like little pricks) pressed feverishly into my chest, her fleecy pubic mound hard against my own hardening prick, her drinking mouth sucking my tongue up as if she meant to draw all of me in, to engulf me, I long just to let myself go, to melt, to flow, to vanish into her forever.

Long ago we dined in the garden of a restaurant where Chinese lanterns were strung in a circle above our heads. They cast a distorting funhouse light on us. We looked at each other through narrowed eyes, each straining to identify the other's face.

But since "long ago" has no actual meaning and can therefore refer to past, present or future, I am always saying, "I have tried." I am always saying, "But I love you." I am always saying, "Do you love me?" And the words always die rushing backward to the time before they were said. Thus we are bemused by colored lights and, falling in love, retreat without moving into the darkness from where I confess that I couldn't live without her; that the thought of her leaving me could drive me mad.

"Don't think it, then," she tells me tartly.

"I would rather kill you than let you go."

"If you kill me," she says (it was then that the world became crowded with shadows, her face a shadow even darker than the rest), "I will return from the grave to haunt you."

"You'll see," she adds. YOU'LL SEE. Future tense, whereby I conclude that, from the beginning, she must have known. Which brings me around again to the

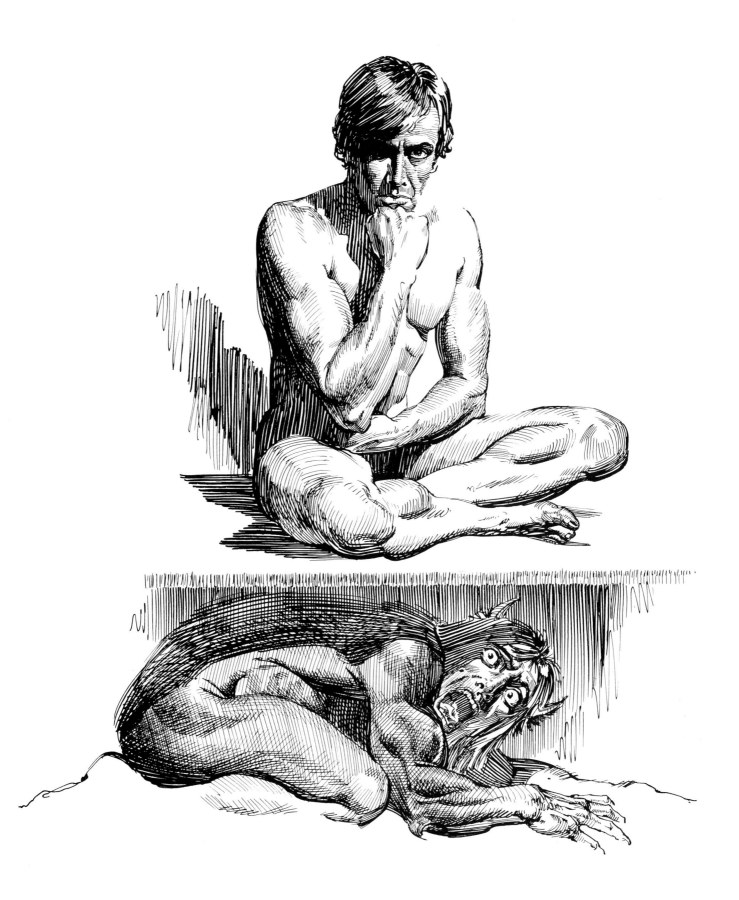

ineluctable question: where to draw the line between the beginning and the absence of a past.

Long ago she left the rooms we shared and returned with a man: slim, narrow shouldered, curly haired; a man with the velvet lips of a woman.

"I met him in a bar. He asked if I'd like a drink and bought me several and also cigarettes and finally said that he'd like to fuck me and I agreed so that's why I've brought him here."

It was treacherous of her to tell me this. She might simply have suggested that I go for a walk. Since she knew this was coming, she could have prepared her little speech with, if not kindness, at least more diplomacy.

Caught without an effective rebuttal, I left without comment.

He was rigorously questioned on this point by two other highly qualified psychiatrists, one called in by the prosecution, one by the defense. The former concluded that he had consciously planned each murder right up to the moment of execution and was motivated by revenge, the need to affirm his masculinity as well as his worth. Clearly, he identified all women with the one that betrayed him. Even so, the battery of clinical tests he was given proved incontestably that he was fully aware of the magnitude and consequences of his acts. He knew where he ended, psychologically speaking, and where the next person began. His perceptions were too much in accordance with the norm and he functioned too well to be considered legally insane.

The defense psychiatrist, however, drew a different conclusion from the tests. He found the defendant's answers and reactions inappropriate for the most part, and wholly indicative of severe paranoia. His connection with reality was tenuous at best. His perception of himself was vastly distorted by chronic feelings of worthlessness, inadequacy, and self-hatred. In short, he was a classic suicidal personality, incapable of sound moral judgment or, indeed, sound judgment of any kind.

At times I behave in a sane fashion. At times I behave insanely. What triggers the insanity? Betrayal is one thing. Fear is another. Fear doesn't have to be defined. We all know what fear is. Betrayal, on the other hand, is subject to interpretation.

That she chose to fuck (or be fucked) by this womanish man is inconsequential. We often agreed that physical fidelity was the mask one wore (A) for public approval and (B) out of consideration for the beloved's ego. It would be absurd to deny that one was attracted to others from time to time. Of course, one could argue

that between the desire and the act it prompts, between the appetite and the eating, so to speak, the "eating" is certainly the greater transgression. Yet we both agreed that sort of quibbling was for pedants, for conformists, for people who lacked the vision to see beyond the facade of stereotypic ethics. No, I don't now and never have presumed to judge her decision to consort with riffraff. She was free to do that. It was purely her affair. But to so crudely throw it in my face, and with such deliberate brutality, that was the consummate betrayal that triggered my (some may call it insane) vengeance.

She didn't much care for the trick I played on her.

"You shitheap!" she screamed, the saliva flying from her mouth. "You crazy fuck!"

"The world of a crazy man is rich," I cheerfully said, "an endlessly fascinating land intricately plotted out between Heaven and Hell."

Her face twisted like a rubber fright mask. Could I yank it off? Was it possible to simply pull off that distorted, hating face and find my lover, my angel, my own sweet girl with the sparkling eyes?

I had watched until they left the apartment and then slunk back, let myself in, waited, and stupidly tormented myself by imagining her with that man, her legs v-spread under him, her mouth open to him, his usurping hands on her breasts, her thighs, her ass; the sweet familiar taste of her cunt on his lips, the honeyed smell of her skin mixing with his sweat.

If he came back with her . . . ? I imagined sinking my fist into his unresistant gut, slamming the heel of my hand down on the back of his neck, and bringing my knee up, fast, cracking the foolish bone of his nose into meaningless splinters.

She returned alone. I heard her clicking steps on the stairs. I stood behind the door, where she could not see me until it was too late. Then I sprang, knocking her aside, slamming the door and locking it.

"Caught like a rat in a trap!" I laughed, happy at her stunned surprise.

I had only intended to keep her there against her will a few days because she hated anything that went against her will. I had only intended to wait until she got hungry enough to beg (with harsh little yelps?) for food so I could give her a few sips of milk and bits of cheese.

I was prepared for her anger and for the crassness of her invective but not for the annihilating coldness in her eyes, not for her physical strength, not for the knife, silver as an icicle, that appeared like a magic wand in her hand. I nearly broke her arm to get it.

A knife does not slice into flesh as into butter. Not even the sharpest knife into the softest, most pliant flesh. There is incredible resistance at first (as if the flesh is mutely crying "NO!") until that appalling give of the breakthrough, the plunge in, the ultimate rape. And then the blood rushes out uncontrollably; the blood erupts as from a live volcano.

I had intended none of this. I only wanted . . . I would have set her free at once, but she was unable to move. Her heart was broken. I took care of her as well as I could. I put a pillow under her head. I stroked her beautiful silken hair. I washed the darkening crimson tears from her face, her body. I kissed and kissed her. I begged her forgiveness, her understanding. She did not answer. Eventually I stopped asking. We were joined to each other by that grim silence.

He was given a pencil and paper in order to record pertinent thoughts that might occur to him between the psychiatric sessions. He wrote nothing. Instead he drew a series of "self-portraits." None of them particularly resembled him. One was of a hollow-eyed little man sitting cross-legged on a cot under which a grinning monster lurked. Another was of an expressionless vacant face and a mask held not quite in front of it, a tragedy mask wrung with unspeakable anguish. There were others, but he destroyed them.

Both the psychiatrist for the defense and the psychiatrist for the prosecution observed that he had considerable artistic talent.

I thought: either she is playing tricks on me or I am playing tricks on myself. She stood behind a counter at Macy's and sold clocks that ticked with inhuman precision. She wore a black turtleneck jersey, striking with her long blond hair. She looked at me with unmistakable recognition.

"How much is this one," I asked, pointing to an exquisitely detailed cuckoo clock. The cuckoo (a gargoyle, in actual fact) seemed monstrously alive.

"That one is not for sale," she answered.

"It looks like a very good clock," I said.

"It tells more than the time," she coolly agreed. "It tells the increasing and decreasing value of life."

"Don't we know each other?" I said. Or perhaps she said it and I remained silent, my heart beating with the same inhuman precision as the cuckoo clock.

We dined in the garden of a restaurant where the dancing light of Chinese lanterns, like funhouse mirrors, distorted our faces.

Long ago, though it was freezing cold, I dripped with hellish burning sweat. It froze at once as I imagined her convulsed with pleasure on the corkscrewing prick of the womanish man. Long ago I confronted her with my anguish, which she could not bear. She cursed me and snapped an icicle from my heart, intent on stabbing me with it. We wrestled. Long ago I won. But since long ago has no actual meaning, it is

the ever-repeating present in which I plunge the icicle through her resistant throat and she backs off shaking: shaking her head as if to deny her guilt, as if to deny against all reason that this is happening, as if to deny that her blood is splashing everywhere: on the walls, on the floor, a rainstorm of rubies . . .

I thought: I am safe now. She must be dead. I was riding in the subway. I was going back and forth from last stop to last stop. She got in at the Fifth Avenue stop. I recognized her at once by her long blond hair. The train jerked and she pretended to stumble against me.

"I'm sorry," she said. Or perhaps I was the one who said I'm sorry. She smiled enigmatically and sat several seats away from me.

The window behind her was open. The wind tore at her hair wildly. She made no attempt to hold it down. When she caught me watching her, she said, "Don't we know each other?" The wind and the roar of the train tangled her words.

The train stopped. I moved to the seat next to her so she could not misunderstand what I had to say. "Don't do this," I told her, outwardly calm. "Don't do it again. Please believe that I am tremendously sorry for everything. And please, please leave me alone."

The train started again. She let herself be jolted against me. Her shoulder pressed mine, an intimacy I might have been happy with once. Blood throbbed at my temples. I was acutely aware of her touch, her hatred, and the crazy pounding of my blood.

"Can you understand me with all this noise?" I asked. I wanted to be perfectly sure.

"I understand that you are afraid of me," she said.

Why couldn't she have said, "You have no reason to be afraid." Why couldn't she have said, "I'm afraid you misunderstand me. I have no intention of hurting you." Because these were lies? I felt the demonic heat of her body next to mine. I felt her moving, breathing so close to me I could hardly persuade myself that I was not reading her thoughts. Still, I might have said to her, "If you can't love me, at least please don't hate me," but I caught sight of myself in the filthy window opposite the seat in which I was slumped: a stunted Goliath with stricken eyes, with the flabby muscles of a has-been gladiator sagging inside his clothes.

"This train stops at Roosevelt Avenue," she said, her face very close to mine. "There we'll have to change for the local."

It seems incredible that I once found her lips sweet.

"I'm not going with you," I blurted, and rushed off before she had time to answer. Thus I lost whatever chance I might have had to talk her out of this scheme of retribution. Perhaps I am a masochist.

At Nedick's, where I gulped a large orangeade, she watched me smilingly from across the street. I escaped into a movie theater. She sat a few rows behind me. I saw her pushing a shopping cart up an aisle toward me at the A & P. For months she pursued me. Even when I did not see her, when I tried to convince myself that she was gone, I could not shake the alarming sense of her presence.

The defendant insisted on pleading not guilty by reason of self-defense. The best arguments against it could not sway him. The jurors were chosen with painstaking care. Two and a half weeks went into the process. No one who had followed the case too closely in the news was acceptable; no one who had formed any opinion as to the actual sanity or insanity of the defendant; no one who expressed anything that might be construed as prejudicial to the case—although it was generally felt (as one man who had been eliminated in the selection bitterly put it): "Those who claim they've got no prejudices are Goddamn liars. If there was such a thing as justice, which there ain't, they'd string up the motherless prick by the balls." Still, the interviews ground hairsplittingly on.

One young woman who faultlessly met all the logic-chopping requirements and had already been accepted by the prosecution was eliminated by one of the attorneys for the defense.

"Call it intuition," he said when he was asked about it. "Something about her makes me uneasy. That long blond hair, you know.... I just don't trust her."

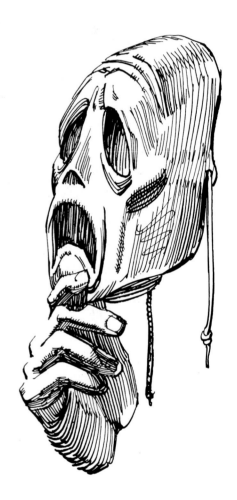

I created this world of blinding darkness. Though I had little choice, I blame no one else. I hide, shivering, in the ragged shadows. I dodge the black lightning lest it strike me in the act of jerkingly living or dying. I am alone, a solitary rabbit fleeing from a demon hound. Therefore, it is up to me to stifle my panic, to decide into which hole I should leapfrog next. And while I'm deciding, I can't help but wonder: Does guilt exist? Or is there merely the absence of innocence? Does absolution exist? Or merely the loss of conscious awareness?

The woman steps from a darkened doorway. "Don't we know each other?" she says. Or perhaps I have said it and she has remained silent. Silence is her element.

"You know you force me to kill you," I say.
Silence is her defense.

"It is the only way I know to save myself."
Silence is her weapon. And a malignant smile. And a thin, sharp, double-edged blade cold as an icicle.

I lunge at her. She sidesteps lightly. Her technique has improved with so much practice. We play the scene

we've played so many times. Lover and beloved: we maul and pound each other. We scald each other with obscenities hot as love vows. We sink and, grunting for breath, rise. We strain in each other's flailing blood-slick arms. Her heartbeat, accelerating in manic tune with my own, is loud as her cries of pleasure in my ears. It stops too suddenly, leaving a silence more shattering than sound. Shocked by that silence, I scream at her.

Her dead eyes stare coldly into mine and the answer I read there, stoic, implacable, charges me with fear.

"Don't!" I howl so loudly that even in death she can't help but hear me. "Don't!"

But her eyes continue their frightful promises.

If I weren't trembling so violently I would press the lids down over those hideous eyes, seal them for good. Yet all I can do is shake and cry uncontrollably—trapped in a puking, fear-cramped body, driven to the brink of lunacy, begging, screaming, promising anything, anything, if only she would leave me, if only she would let me go.

I have no idea how long I raved until I found the presence of mind and the strength to run . . . to run . . . Yet, in the streets or in my room, at the grocer's or the butcher's or at the movies, talking, eating, laughing, shouting, pounding the walls, pounding my head against the walls, awake, asleep, alive, or dead she will pursue me, an indefatigable bloodhound, my stench in her quivering nostrils forever.

The much-publicized case never came to court. The day the young blond woman was dismissed as a prospective juror, the defendant was found dead in his cell. Suicide was ruled out almost immediately because of the savage stabbing he had sustained. It was physically impossible for him to have administered such wounds. The murder weapon was never found. Nor the murderer.

Considerable speculation surrounded the large icicle that was discovered melting near the body. How could an icicle materialize in a locked jail cell in ninety-degree weather? Some thought it had to be the missing weapon. Others dismissed this idea as thoroughly outlandish. And even if it was the weapon, they argued, who or what could have managed to slip past the twenty-four-hour maximum security system with what must have been (judging by the size of the puddle in which it was found) a four-foot icicle in tow?

Satisfactory conclusions were never reached.

The state prosecutor, when asked his off-the-record opinion, shrugged his shoulders.

ENCHANTMENT

Paradoxically, it was the newer wing of the house that collapsed. The old wing (about which there were always such warnings: *the floor is paper thin, be careful...*), with its labyrinthian hallways and intersecting rooms, endures unchanged. As if in denial that anything has happened. But the unalterable fact is that it has happened.

Sometimes I have trouble remembering exactly what things were like before the collapse. Whole portions of my life seem to have been blown away like snow by the wind to settle, cold and white, in some untrammeled region. Trauma, I know, can cause partial amnesia. So I don't consider my case too unusual.

I might have been lying on the bed, my eyes closed, when it began. I might have been trying to go to sleep: imagining my feet getting heavy, feeling the heaviness move upward, when I heard the first portentous shiftings and rumblings.

Or I might have been standing in front of a mirror, studying my face: dark, dream-haunted eyes gazing out of a pale face wreathed by white-blond hair. My most striking feature is my hair. When I turn my head from side to side, it flashes like quicksilver.

I might just as well have been standing at the window when I heard it. The uncurtained casement window, through which I had a perfect view of the slowly encroaching woods, is quite clear in my mind. The trees, which at one time bordered fifteen acres of velvet lawn, had unremittingly edged closer over the years. Now they form a veritable jungle fortress around what is left of the house.

I must admit that, for a time, their uninhibited growth intrigued me. I pretended that the house was an enchanted castle and that I, its princess, awaited the prince who must fight his way through all that savagely flourishing vegetation to find me. But that was years ago. These days the sight of it is only an irritation.

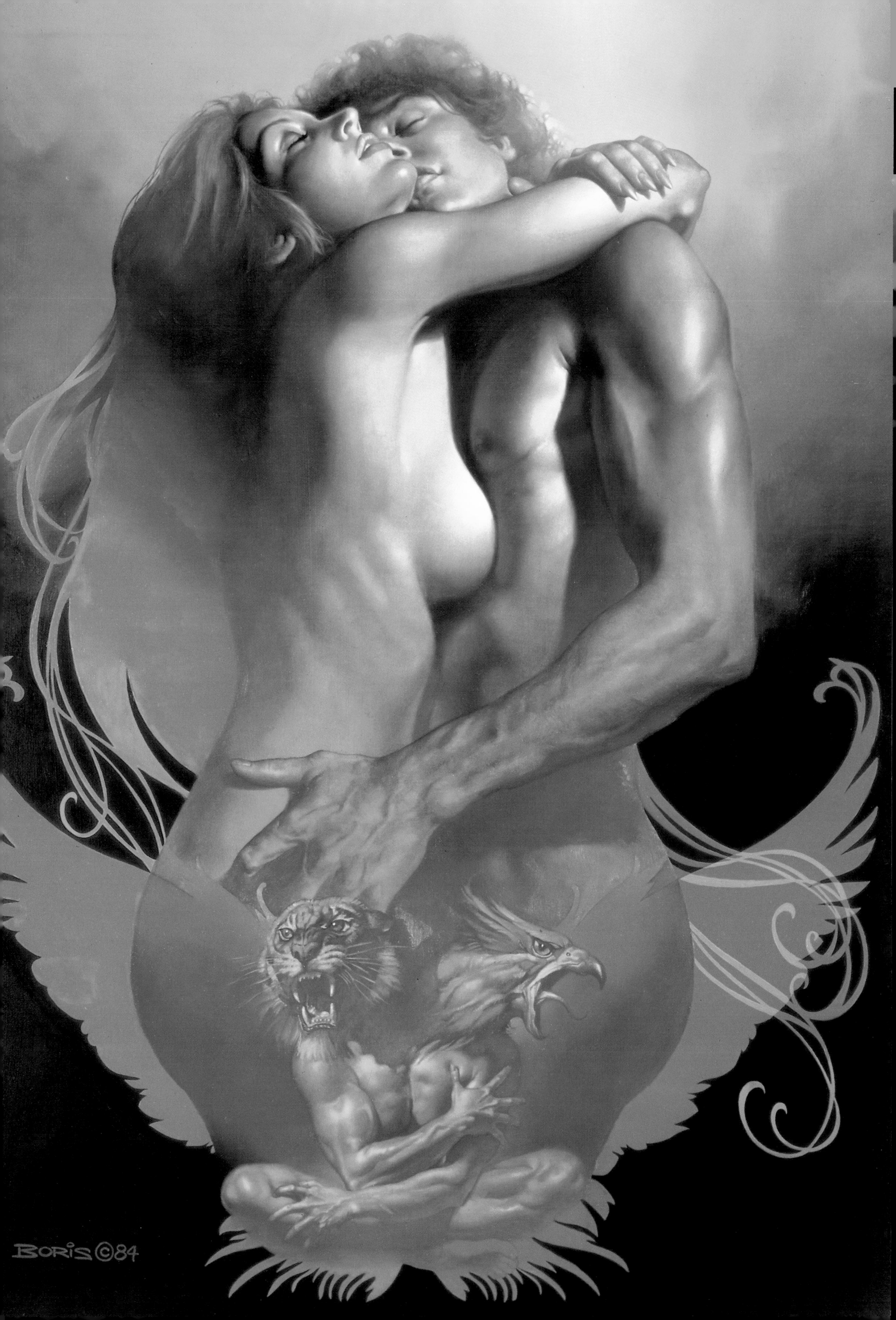
BORIS ©84

I wonder why they never did anything about that wilderness, those dolts who hammered and hacked at the house with such lunatic glee. "This will be the living room," they trilled, cutting a muraled ballroom in half. "And this other part will be the garage." The mural, a hunt scene with men in glorious red coats and black-gowned ladies riding sidesaddle, was pulled off the wall and left lying on the ground for weeks. When the plastering and painting began, it served as a drop cloth.

Possibly I was sitting in a chair just gazing at the wall when it happened. Possibly I was gazing at nothing, my mind empty, when the sound so like a growl of thunder presaged the imminent collapse. What I do remember is that the walls of my former bedroom were painted yellow, an undaunted buttercup yellow. Of all the rest—as of a dream after waking—I am uncertain.

I was sitting or lying or standing in the yellow bedroom when I understood, suddenly, that the house was collapsing. As in a dream, where madness can seem remarkably sane, I had no special urge to run. That I might be killed by the falling rubble posed only a distant threat. Far more immediate was the heaviness in my limbs that impeded the slightest effort to move. It seemed to me I could put escape off for a while. This I did, too, until the crumbling plaster fell like hail and stung my body into motion.

I remember how a whole section of the forest surprisingly appeared where the wall had been. And I remember shielding my head with my arms, the plaster dust drying my tears. The plaster dust was everywhere, in my nostrils, my hair, my clothes, even in my underwear. It stuck in patches to my skin. I remember thinking it would take me years to wash it all away.

I blame it all on them. They weakened the basic structure of the house with their callous renovations. At least they left after that. I haven't seen them again, which is fine with me. It is possible they put what was left of the house up for sale and haven't interested any buyers. It is also possible that they preferred simply to forget about it (though how they could do this with property taxes as a yearly reminder is beyond me). I don't know. I don't want to know. I moved into the older surviving wing.

The house, situated on one of the many hills that ring Putnam Valley, was built nearly two hundred years ago. The first owners bred horses, I heard. A moldering barn still stands some distance off in the woods.

From its incongruous appearance, it is apparent that the original house—stone walled and much more cohesive in design—had been augmented at various intervals, probably as the children of the nuclear family married and had children of their own. Whole suites had been added with a capricious disregard for archi-

tectural precepts or consistency in style. Parts were finished in brick, parts in shingle, parts in wood. Some areas were stuccoed, others done with cement blocks.

Once I was shown some faded blueprints for the house. They reminded me of charts in an anatomy textbook: an uncanny skeleton and the convoluted pathways of its veins and arteries. The blueprints disclosed a secret wine cellar behind a sliding wall panel in the library. Small, damp, and thick with cobwebs, it proved singularly disappointing. The rusty pipes near its ceiling had leaked and the wines stored and forgotten there had, without exception, turned to vinegar.

I mention the wine cellar only because it was hidden, a secret built into the foundation of the house. Though the blueprints betrayed no other secrets, no other hidden doors, vaults, or stairways, the existence of secrets was implicit in the very eccentricity of these designs. It is the only explanation for the enigmatic visits that began (to the best of my recollection) after the cave-in.

I was sitting in the kitchen. It is large by today's standards—twenty-five feet in length and about half that in width. A row of windows facing east on the long side presents the view of a garden overgrown by weeds. I do think weeds have their own special beauty. Snapdragons, bluebells, Queen Anne's lace; I pick them sometimes. They make appealing bouquets. I had, in fact, just brought such a bouquet into the kitchen, put it in water, and set it on the table when I experienced the strangest sense of expectancy.

As if I were waiting for someone, all the sounds —and in an old house there are many—took on acute meaning. Footsteps, were they? Breathing? I wasn't sure who I was waiting for. Or if the kitchen was the place to wait. Wouldn't it be better to receive a visitor in the living room? Or in the garden? Perhaps near the fountain with its replica of the splendidly irreverant "Maniken Piss," that angelic-faced boy from whose tiny stone penis water still spouted gurglingly into the shell-shaped basin in which it stood.

I arose and passed through the living room with its stone fireplace and dark carpets out into the dazzle of the garden. A butterfly, a brilliant black and orange monarch, fluttered away from its perch on an abandoned lawn chair. Some presence—not mine—had alarmed it. I was distinctly aware of someone having just passed there ahead of me, of a whisper having just faded to silence.

Was the phantom real or imaginary? Should I go looking for him? (I glimpsed a movement among the abundantly blooming honeysuckle where, had he remained motionless, he would have had no more reality than an intoxicatingly fragrant shadow.) Should I dismiss him as insubstantial?

And if I found him?

I wanted to find him every bit as much as I knew that I must not look too hard. I must not burst into empty rooms or turn my head too suddenly. To see him would be to break some mysterious pledge, some half-remembered bond between us.

He did become my lover, visiting me first—as such enchanters do—while I slept, his embraces mingling with my dreams. I would awake with the fleeting illusion of having made love to myself as once, long ago, when I pressed my lips against those of my mirror image. But this mystical lover, warm, malleable, and ever indistinct, was not locked behind glass.

I would awaken with the feeling of his lips on my breasts, with the echo of his "I love you" like rustling grass near my head.

I would awaken with a vague sensation of loss.

For a long time I would lie perfectly still, absorbing the night that pressed against me. The phosphorescent moonlight flowing through the window transformed all shapes into phantoms. My marabou-trimmed robe flung over the back of a bentwood chair became the head and ruffed neck of a bird, its enormous lugubrious eyes ever watchful, its beak startlingly phallic. The armchair and ottoman (from which the fringed edging had, in part, torn loose) became a beast, half man, half lion. His lazily stirring tail, rendered partly invisible by the darkness, ended there where my fingertips tapped at the gradually swelling prune pit of flesh between my legs.

I would imagine the room to be a cave in which I was a prisoner. The window became the mouth of the cave and blazed with silvery light that, whenever I approached, darkened at once.

My lover guarded the mouth of the cave, blocking it with his body when I tried to leave. I never saw all of him. He was too large to be entirely visible from in here. Thus I didn't know him entirely but only his sexual organ, which he introduced through the cave's entrance. This organ was like an elephant's trunk: thick, strong, exquisitely sensitive.

It was a magic wand.

The game of captive and guard excited me. I enjoyed creeping slyly toward the mouth of the cave to see if I couldn't give him the slip. Knowing he would anticipate my move heightened the challenge. I inched my way toward him carefully, carefully. I crept, flattened against the ground, hardly daring to think lest the soundless dance of my thoughts alert him. Still, he was ready, always ready, his hard, direct elephant's trunk always driving me back.

I had no idea of his name or his actual shape. Yet with each newly discovered clue—each caress, each sighed endearment—I felt that my discovery had taken place before.

I tried to convince myself that this was all right. That there was no more need to identify him than to analyze the function of love. That it didn't matter whether I actually saw him or only dreamed him. That no cause would be served by transforming him from enchanted prince into ordinary man or, worse, into nothing. And yet, my anxieties increased. A nightmare, terrible and beautiful, hovered above me on steadily beating wings.

It became essential for me to know him, to assure myself of his solidity. I wanted to anchor myself to safety through him. The need obsessed me. The longing to know him went to the heart, to the bone marrow. It began to feel more like an illness I ought to try to recover from than like love.

The best thing to do, I decided, was to occupy myself productively; not to think of him at all; not to spend my time wondering who he was or when or where he would come to me again. Despite all this, I found myself catching sight of him in doorways, in shadows, in a curtain blowing at an open window—everywhere where he turned out not to be.

Once, awakened by a sound I took to be his step, I arose and ran from the bedroom to the stairs. There he was, a single burning candle in his hand, climbing upward out of a sinister darkness that lay thick as a fog below. He looked incredibly thin, nearly transparent, bent, as if with pain, under the effort of dragging himself toward me. For a moment he rested. Or was he deciding whether or not to go back down? The small flame threw a shifting light on his face and continually recast his features: youthful, ancient, coarse, tragic, unendurably sensitive.... Who was he?

The darkness congealed, obliterating the foot of the staircase. I reached out to grasp his free hand, to help him up the last few steps. Shadows snatched at me, struck at me like storm-whipped branches, but it was he who was abruptly pulled away. His candle guttered and went out. A large black mouth swallowed him up.

Later on I wondered if he had not staged that scene deliberately, appeared helpless so I would rush to save him, but that, in fact, he had no intention of letting me get the upper hand. By never appearing when or where I expected him to and by keeping his identity a mystery, he stoked both my longings and my apprehensions.

All love is obsessive, no less so the love that pains and exhausts. To mitigate his spell, I decided to find someone else. I went into town with this express intention.

At the Eagle's Nest I met a man in his early thirties. He was attractive in spite of his habit of staring unflinchingly into my eyes as if to convince me, by force, of his sincerity. His deep-set brown eyes under their heavy brows, suggestive of a tempestuous nature, were offset by a vagueness about the rest of his face. It seemed slightly blurred, as if seen from too great a distance to be dependably real.

The apartment to which he took me was a single sparsely furnished room. Its only two windows, near the ceiling, were at street level. He offered me a whiskey, which I accepted.

As we took our clothes off, the room gradually shrank. The windows became slits and the reduced light faded everything to shades of gray. When he came toward me, he also shrank until his mouth was vis-à-vis my sex, which he kissed once quickly. It seemed to me he felt obliged to do this or risk appearing inexperienced but that, at the same time, he found it somewhat distasteful.

On the way to the bed he passed through a shaft of street light, and his steel-gray skin looked nearly white. In contrast, the wiry hairs, disconcertingly dense on his legs and chest, had the appearance of matted fur. Having come this far, though, I reasoned, I might as well see the whole business through. The fact of infidelity, if not the act, would bring me a measure of satisfaction. Let's get it over with then, I thought, as he reared above me, hoisting his penis like the barrel of a gun.

The sun was just setting as I returned. The air was still warm. I decided to have a light dinner in the garden. As soon as I emerged from the house with my

bowl of mixed fruit and milk, I sensed my lover's presence. However, I pretended not to. I sat near the manikin fountain and ate my fruit leisurely. When I finished, I set my bowl aside and lay back in the grass, my arms behind my head and my eyes closed.

So, he had missed me.

So, due to my afternoon's absence, he was no longer that certain of me. I stretched, yawned, and, in a while, affected the regular deep breathing of sleep. The cicadas, which at this hour usually trilled their insistent love calls, were still. Did I start falling asleep? Pictures I could not quite get into focus kept floating to the surface. I had an impression of myself as existing in a dimension other than the obvious one. In this other dimension I was light, buoyant, hollow-boned as a bird. I could bound over the surrounding hills, I could ride great updrafts of air clear to the sky. Amphibian-lunged, I could play the games of starfish and minnows. I could read the ripples on the ocean floor and understand the language of forgotten bones.

The stillness in the garden began to develop a dimension of its own out of which images, like dream fragments, kept materializing. My lover, hidden in the statue of the manikin, watched me. I felt the deep concentration with which he sought to penetrate my dream. He had no idea that I was not asleep. I could catch him now, leap up and grab the round-cheeked cherub inside which he crouched, cut off his escape and demand to know who he was and what he meant by his maddening games of hide and seek. However, I did not.

A sparkling jet of water arced from the manikin's tiny phallus into the stone shell. The arc wavered, rose and fell, gurgled, sputtered, and streamed forth again, this time overshooting the edge of the fountain and wetting my legs.

"I missed you," he whispered. The words were water surging across my thighs. "Missed you... missed... you..." The stream rushed over me. I drank his words. I let them flood me, let them tear me unresistingly along.

One's name spoken aloud, even casually, softly, is often enough to rouse one from dreams. And how disorienting it can be to open one's eyes too suddenly, the sense of what was still real a moment before already fading as a new reality one is dismayingly unprepared for rams itself against the consciousness. You are not too sure where you are or, perhaps, even what you are. You may have the illusion of observing yourself through the eyes of a distinctly separate being while at the same time remaining wholly uncertain which of you is real and which is only the ghostly residue of the dream.

I was lying on a grassy expanse of field. Or was it the bare dirt I was lying on? Was it a hard floor? Or was it, in reality, a closed and windowless room, a sepulcher in which the darkness was a broad hand flattened against my eyes? I could feel the movements of my lover, his shifting, his body rising. I could hear people talking. They passed nearby.

At first I hadn't the slightest idea what to do. It was obvious I couldn't just lie there while strangers wandered about the property. I should at least get up and see who they were, although the temptation to remain concealed was almost overwhelming. Clearly, they hadn't seen me. And something of the vague danger I constantly feared lay in pursuing them. But I heard my name mentioned again.

A woman's voice was telling about the collapse of the newer part of the house and how the old house, built around the mid eighteen hundreds, was still quite sound, really quite solidly put together...

I plunged into my new disconcerting wakefulness, forced my eyes open, and again open.

A man and a woman were walking toward the house. They looked indistinct, as though seen through

mist. Were they real? If I dreamed them gone, would they vanish? They seemed to have no weight, no density. The woman was slender and wore a beige dress. Her companion, considerably taller than she, wore a pale blue shirt and darker slacks. He carried a briefcase in one hand. I darted after them.

Distances became deceiving. I almost ran into the woman as she fussed with the lock of the front door. I stopped just in time. They entered the narrow vestibule with its shadows and mysteries. I slipped in behind them, dimly aware that my lover, too, followed.

"Here, to the left, is the living room," the woman said. "The fireplace works rather well, so I'm told, which can be a considerable saving on the heat bill. In a house this size, as you might imagine, that can be

substantial in winter time. Naturally, you can always close off those rooms you don't need, which would be an additional saving."

The man answered that economy concerned him less, particularly at this time of the year, than privacy.

"You'll get nothing if not privacy," the woman said. "This place is given wide berth by folks around here."

"So I've heard," the man answered and, after a pause, added, "I've never seen a ghost, actually. Quite frankly, I would like to sometime."

The woman laughed softly. "Maybe you'll be in luck. The ones that supposedly haunt this place are a brother and sister. They're supposed to be twins, I believe, who died here at the time."

Another's hand laid, even gently, on your shoulder is often enough to dispel the dream. And how bewildering to turn with the knowledge of what you will see already thrusting itself against your vehement denials: the world, which was still safely insulated a moment before, already stripped bare and mercilessly cold. It may occur to you that you knew all along but preferred to lock up this knowledge as one might lock up a house before leaving.

I felt my lover's light touch on my shoulder and I remembered him already. I turned as his face bloomed out of my memory like an image out of the mysterious depthlessness of a mirror, my face, and yet, unmistakably his: the firmer jawline ending, however, in the same impudent thrust of chin; the broader forehead wreathed by the same silver-bright hair; the same oblique darkly luminous eyes, only larger.

I should have looked away, fallen asleep, searched out again that other dimension in which he had no name, no real identity. But the disruption of that dream had brought him too close. We stared at each other, my brother and I, until the corners of his mouth, curving into a sad, defiant smile, began to tug at my own.

FULL MOON

Still wearing the ripped T-shirt and faded blue jeans from the night before, he rolled gingerly from his stomach to his back. The room lurched along with him. He groaned, cursed, and lay still. His right arm dangled over the side of the bed. His eyes were closed against the thin blades of light filtering between the slats of the venetian blind. Spears of light cut through his closed lids.

Outside, a car stopped, its radio blasting. A rock and roll beat divebombed at his head. "Shit," he murmured, his skull exploding with light and noise. All his thoughts had gone *pfffft*, blown away by the goddamn sunlight and the maniac with the radio. "Get the fuck out of here," he said softly, pleadingly. The car moved on. The music dimmed into uneasy silence. What did he do last night?

Why were his teeth chattering?

Why was he drenched in sweat? shivering?

What memory stalked him?

A muscle twitched in his right leg. In his calf. He had no control over it. It might be a snake moving under his skin. But if there was a snake somewhere, it was not in his leg. If there was a snake it was in his head, moving silently as a lighthouse beam searching through fog.

What did he do last night?

The TV was off in the next room. Had the Warden gone out? Gone to work? What time was it? Maybe she'd gotten herself a job delivering concrete blocks. She had the face for it: flap mouth, fat ass, drooping boobs the shape of bombs. *Bombers*, he'd called them during one of their rare moments of loving. "You could snuff a guy just by laying one of those bombers of yours across his face."

She had been the only one to visit him in the can. She had waited for him.

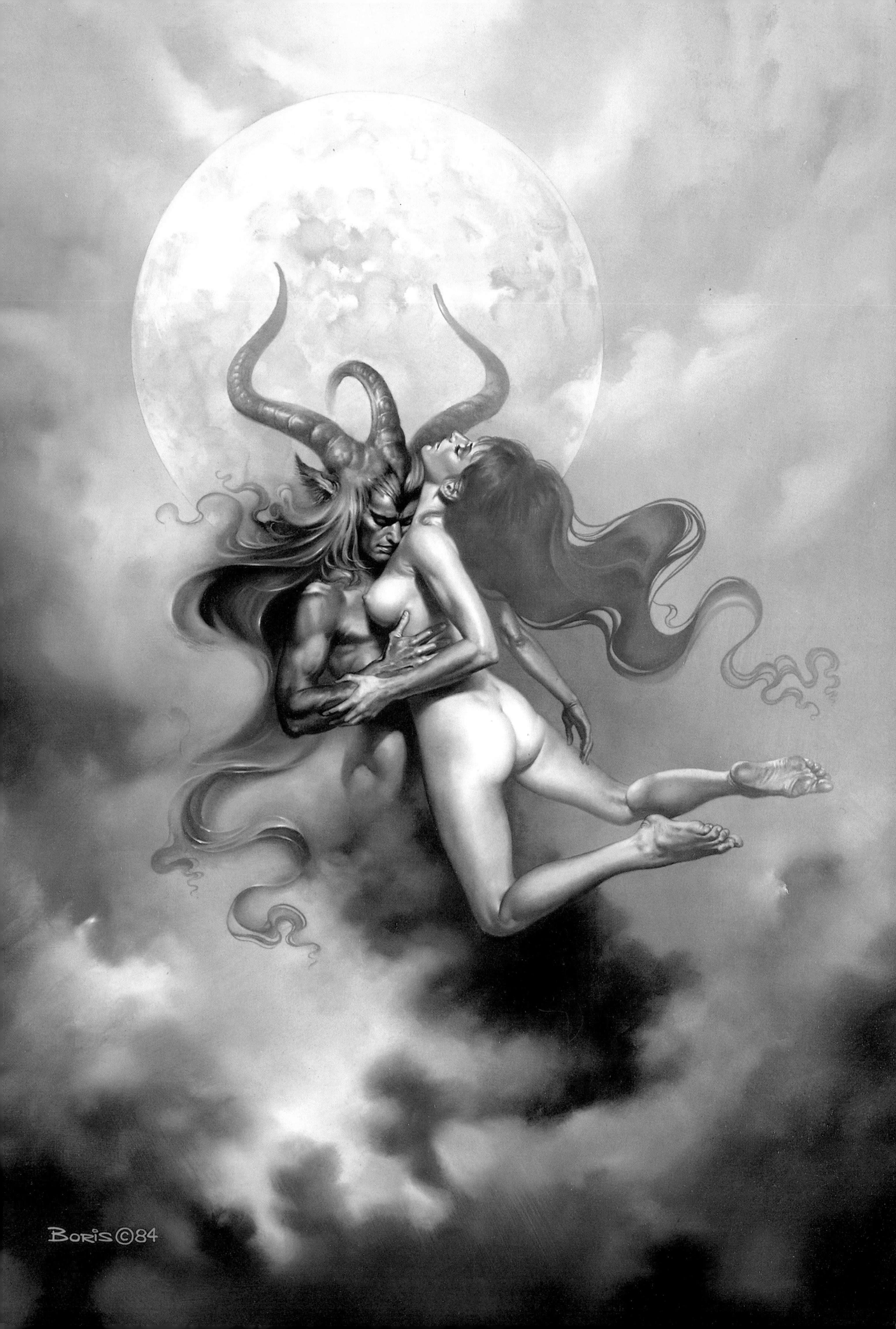
BORIS ©84

She had let him stay at her place when he had no-where to sleep but in his car, no address other than good old Hotel Buick. And, except for a dozen or so times, he hadn't repaid her. Not in the way she wanted.

Was that his fault?

"Do you care for me?" she'd ask him over and over.

"Sure, babe, I'm nuts about you." The lie came easily enough. And maybe it wasn't a hundred percent lie. He had repaid her a dozen or so times, when he'd been really shit-faced.

Who was to blame that he had trouble getting a hard-on with her?

Two warm tears slipped from his closed eyes to trickle into his hair. His eyes always teared when he was hung over. *What did he do last night?*

Had there been a full moon?

The searchlight in his head cut through the fog. He knew well enough what he must have done. Nothing he had not done before. Or would not do again. No mystery. He just did not want to deal with it first thing on waking.

It is a statistically proven fact that police stations, hospital emergency rooms, and those hot-shot places that have doorknobs on the outside of their doors only, all do a rip-roaring business on full moon nights. So…

Is what happens to him really strange? Really freaky? Probably not. Probably there are others like him who sometimes dream dreams to go crazy by.

The first time he saw the full moon high in the sky, it was sleeping, a small, curled-up thing too far off to matter. Too far off to touch or be touched by. It seemed. But it tricked him. It slid slowly and so slyly down the black sky he hardly noticed it getting larger and brighter. He watched. He got stoned on watching, stoned on wondering if it was falling toward him or he was falling toward it.

And while he was still wondering, it stepped light as a cat through his window to stand—no longer small or too far away—in his room. Not ten feet from him. Sizing him up with silver eyes. Its eyes made the deepest impression. They appeared to be almost independent of the thing. They illuminated the entire room. Twin burning moons, they filled the whole world with a beautiful scary light.

What he did last night was lock the door between himself and the Warden, who, anyway, was watching TV. What he did was open the window. What he did was dream of a creature alighting on the sill and fold-ing its great crystalline wings in a gesture of unmistak-able intent. Since parts of the dream still seemed awfully real, parts of it might have happened. The crea-ture could have had gleaming skin that, with the slight-est shift of the light, turned into short, glossy fur. Had horns curved from its head? Had nostrils flared in a darkly silken muzzle? He couldn't swear to it. But he did remember the teeth, ivory white and strong, and the tongue lolling wetly between them.

"Catch," the apparition had shouted. It removed its head and flung it directly at him. The head, turning round and round in the air, landed against his chest with a hollow thunk. His hands involuntarily reached to catch it. The apparition laughed, and its laugh had all the intangible sweetness of a lover's whisper. How could it have laughed without a head? But it had a head. A full moon glowed silvery bright on its neck.

His bones grew soft. Desire flickered at last to life in the cold crannies of his body. When he looked down at the head cradled in his arms, it was flaccid, empty, a rubber Halloween mask. He put it on without think-ing and became something else. A wild excitement licked through his veins. He sprang lightly onto the window ledge and unfolded his wings.

Once he puts on the mask, the transformation is predictable as death. Once he lets the full moon into his window… *I will not let it happen. I will not let it happen. I will not let it happen…*, he wrote, covering five sheets of paper on both sides. He tried keeping the window closed. Keeping the blinds closed. Watch-ing TV with the Warden. Putting an arm around her, for whatever that was worth. When was the last time he actually laid a hand on her arm or her shoulder?

There might even be a way to not let it happen. Only, he hasn't found it yet.

Last night…

Why, he didn't even know the woman. Not her name. Not where she came from. Not how old she was. She looked sixteen or seventeen under the warpaint, the white leather miniskirt, the bikini top out of which her melons bulged. A runaway, probably from East Punkville or some such live spot.

"Wanna have fun, sweetheart?" she said.

His need, alive and hungering for some time, grew enormous. Hard as he was, he could have taken her right there on Thirty-ninth Street, pounded himself into her doggie fashion, drilled into her like a jackhammer.

"How much, love?" he asked, his voice coming from deep in his throat.

"Twenty-five," she said, already fearful behind her smile. "And twenty for the room."

"You got it." He recognized her fear as something they shared.

"Do you love me," the Warden murmured between insistent kisses. "Sure, babe, sure," he answered as, inside of himself, he withdrew.

Careful to dodge the streetlights, he loped after the young hooker. It would not do for her to get too good a look at him, to pick up too soon on what he was.

She had nice round buns, he noted as he followed her up the stairs. In a minute he'd have his hands on them. In a minute he'd be riding high. In a minute she'd be bucking and whooping under him. Or maybe she'd be lying dead-assed under him, like a store window dummy, waiting for the squirt between her legs to pick up and go hunting again.

As he would go hunting.

"I don't know the answer," he said to the Warden when (not tearfully, but as close to tears as she ever came) she wanted him to "Please just explain why. *Why!*" "Maybe it's all the years I spent in the can without women. With just the women in my head. Just the pictures of movie stars cut out of magazines. All the stuff that happened to me there...Maybe I'm trying to make up for lost time. I don't know." Which wasn't exactly true. He did know. At least in part. What happened happened because of the full moon. What he did then he did because he was not real, because full-moon time was a time separate from real life, a time when shadows grew Cheshire Cat faces with hungry mouths and eyes that were tunnels to sweet hell.

What he truly could not explain was why, instead of climbing quietly back through his window as usual, he had come lumbering drunkenly through the front door on that particular night, reeking of the evening, his pants cum stained, his shirt torn.

He never knows any of the women. Maybe that's why he loves them. Maybe, too, that is some part of the explanation. If it is, though, it is just so much worthless information, because it doesn't change anything. Not that he cares much, anymore, to change anything. In real life he is a failed thief, a failed forger, a failed lover, a general fuck-up. When the full moon hits, he is the eighth wonder of the world. He is Superman! With the moonlight burning in his gut he can score faster than a speeding bullet, he can leap over the tallest pricks with a single bound, he can keep humping for ever and ever.

Do you like it this way, love?
Crazy, Crazy. It's driving me crazy....

He met her at the Club Hypnotique, a glittering barn of a place. The first thing he spotted in the gyrating mob was her spun-sugar hair. It was the color of orange Popsicles and he wanted her like mad. So, wading into the crush of dancers, he edged bump by grind closer to her until he was less than an arm's length away. The strobe lights flashed and flashed, snapping her at him—her clown-white face with its eyes like bruises—snatching her away, snapping her back, snatching her away while she shook and swayed to the electronic heartbeat that effaced her and jerked her back to life instant after instant.

Outside the Club, streetlights glinted in her hair like smoldering stars. He put his arm around her waist, the crashing pulse of the music still in his ears. She towered over him, a giantess in red spandex jeans and a sleeveless, almost backless, red blouse. She had the tail of a lioness, long and slender, with a bushy tip. It switched back and forth as she walked. She had touchingly small bluebird wings folded against her shoulder blades. He found the combination of blue and red a bit corny against her white skin.

"It don't bother you none?" she asked, meaning her height.

"Hell no, babe," he said, his eyes on her spandex crotch. "I'm just as good at going up as getting on down."

She laughed a booze-husky bray. "Oh, man, that kills me. That freaking kills me!"

The red jeans peeled off like ripe banana skins, and her legs were long and powerful as a wrestler's. She flipped them over his shoulders. She got him in a headlock between her thighs. He drank her scent. He got drunk on it; the feral musk of a bitch in heat. She pressed her palms against the tips of his horns. She rubbed her hands up and down on them, stroking, stroking.

"Don't forget to come up for air, lover." Her voice was a low, raw laugh.

He was happy as a back-alley tomcat. He wallowed in her: in the taste of her, in the smell of her, in her heat, in the feel of her legs around his neck.

The Warden knew and didn't know what he was. What she must have discovered, if she knocked on the door when he locked it between them, was that there'd be no answer. Had she ever unlocked the door to find the window open and the room empty? She never exactly said anything.

But...

One morning he found her slumped in her TV-watching chair.

"Good morning, merry sunshine," he said.

No response from her. He repeated his greeting. No response. He lifted her arm and let it go. It fell limply. It swung back and forth like a pendulum. Her head dropped forward onto her chest, and he panicked. He frantically began to shake her. He was suddenly on the verge of laughing or crying or dying because he thought she was dead.

She opened her eyes and said, "Fun, isn't it, when the shoe is on the other foot?"

That she could do this to him... That she would do this... He felt very bad. Very low. He said he was sorry from the depths of his crazy heart. He said he would never not answer her again when she knocked. Never leave her. Never ever give her cause to wish she were dead. Or he was dead. And he was willing to do anything to prove he meant this. Anything to change his ways. What the hell, he was sick and tired of waking up sick and tired, sad, secretive, drained, guilty, half mad. She wanted him to go to Sunday Mass. She said it would help. Tough luck that she was wrong.

It was the statue of the Virgin that screwed everything up. By having the Warden's long-suffering cow eyes that said: Your fault! It's all your fault! You shit!

He sat in his pew and looked down at his hands and continued to hear the cow eyes saying: You owe me, kiddo! For all the crap you have put me through!

So he stared at the rows of white flames in red glasses and thought: Okay, babe, whatever you say. And he tried to shut out the visions of dancing silver moons.

"What is it? Are you sick?" the Warden asked.

He had started to cough. The cough turned into

choking. He was trying to shut out the feel of thighs clamping down on his neck. "Nothing," he croaked. "Just an itch at the back of my throat." But the scent of all those burning candles filled his lungs. He knew candles didn't smell like hungry cunts. Just as he knew that whoever carved the statue didn't have the Warden in mind. Just as he knew that stone eyes didn't speak. He tried to stay cool. To think about how it would all be over soon. Then the priest began his rap about guilt and redemption, and he charged out of there like a wounded bull.

What he did last night filled him with fear on the edge of terror, terror on the edge of joy, joy blasting through him like blood-red cherry bombs.

The woman told him her name was Lorelei. He knew it wasn't her real name, that she only pretended to be Lorelei because they all did. He bought her a brandy with a Coke chaser and ordered a beer for himself.

She wore a heart-shaped locket on a thin gold chain around her neck. It was the kind in which there is space for a tiny picture. She told him there was no picture inside. Nevertheless, she would not let him open it.

"I want you to put my picture in there," he said.

"How much will that set me back?"

"Twenty bucks for a hand job, thirty to blow you, forty for a straight lay, fifty for sixty-nine, and up from there depending on what you want and what you want to spend on it." She had pouting lips, golden curls, full, red cheeks like a cherub's. But what made him love her was the icy glitter of her blue eyes, all the more compelling because it hinted of desperation close to the surface. The frozen brilliance of those blue eyes blew his mind.

After all the promises, the regrets, and the good intentions, the light of the full moon still controlled him, would control him, would reach him even through closed windows and drawn blinds. Any struggle he might launch against it, any struggle he had ever launched against it, always failed. Always would fail. What was the use of promises?

What he did last night was lock the door, paint the window black from top to bottom so not the thinnest ray of light could shine through, smoke cigarettes, maybe a hundred of them, until the air was gray and bitter with smoke. He lay down on the bed, got up, paced back and forth in the room, drank beer, lay down again, and continued drinking, determined not

to move from the bed. Not to move from the room. To steel himself against it and to long for the agony of it to purge him, to break the spell, to change him once and for always into a free man.

He had not counted on the power of the moon. It sought him out from behind his painted windows. It carried more than brilliance, it had power and force. Under its weight the black paint began to flake and the small motes of pigment burst into the air. The moon became a thousand tantalizing stars projected deep into the room through a crazy glass. He had not counted on the pinpoints of moonlight condensing, dewlike, on his skin. Changing the texture of his skin, changing even the structure of the bones that skin covered.

What he did last night was give Lorelei sixty dollars he had lifted from the Warden's purse. That was the price for opening her heart-shaped locket. Inside there was a tiny heart-shaped mirror in which, as he moved it slightly this way and that, he could glimpse the sharp tip of a horn, the wet gleam of a muzzle, the glint of an inhuman eye, the dark edge of a wing.

"I love you," she said in the voice of a porcelain cherub. "I love the thickness of your fur, the size of your horns, the roughness of your paws against my skin, the strength in those gigantic wings of yours. We can fuck and fly at the same time, darling, and it will only cost you ten dollars more."

Her sweet mechanical words rushed to his groin. He could hardly wait to tear off her clothes, to bury himself in her, to be huge in her, to devour her, to re-create her.

"Cross my palm with silver first," she said.

Oh, he was wild about her. He gave her all the money he had and they flew high over the city of plastic houses and toy cars and windup dolls, fucking all the way up and all the way down again. And when it was over he loped home through the streets like a man on an opium high, hardly aware of the traffic, the tourists, the citizens, the peddlers, the human and animal strays that faded in and out past him.

The TV still sounded when he climbed back through the window. Was she watching? Was she asleep in front of it? If he went in to turn it off, would she play dead? Would she play at all? He closed the window, lowered the blinds, lay down, and waited to change back before he went in. The moon was almost gone. It wouldn't take long. But while he was waiting, he fell asleep.

SPHINX

"I do feel that perhaps you did not ask the correct questions of the Sphinx."

"What would you ask?"

"I would not be concerned with the secrets, the lies, the mysteries, the facts. I would be concerned with *what makes them necessary.* What fear?"

—*The Diary of Anaïs Nin*

The Sphinx lies on her side, her head resting on her folded arms, her tail swishing back and forth. The Lion Trainer enters the ring. The audience applauds. He has a burning hoop in one hand and, in the other, a whip, which he cracks. The Sphinx rises to her haunches. He cracks the whip again and she leaps through the flames.

The audience applauds.

He extinguishes the fire, discards the hoop, and bows. The sequins on his satin shirt glitter and flash. If she would always obey her cues as she has just done, his life would be easier. Unfortunately, half beast that she is, her performance is never predictable. Nor her moods. She can waken from a perfectly peaceful sleep with her eyes ready to draw blood, her lips a snarl over murderous teeth. She can plunge into a mournful languor after the most successful performance. To praise her at such times is to elicit sighs that seem to arise out of unendurable sadness.

He considers her potentially dangerous. She could, he knows, effortlessly eviscerate him. The trick is not to let her discover this. He has been tempted to use tranquilizers on her—a routine tool for some trainers. Thus far he has not. He thinks there would be no satisfaction in training a sedated sphinx and is proud of how far he has come with her.

She was afraid of the fire and he told her there was nothing to be afraid of,

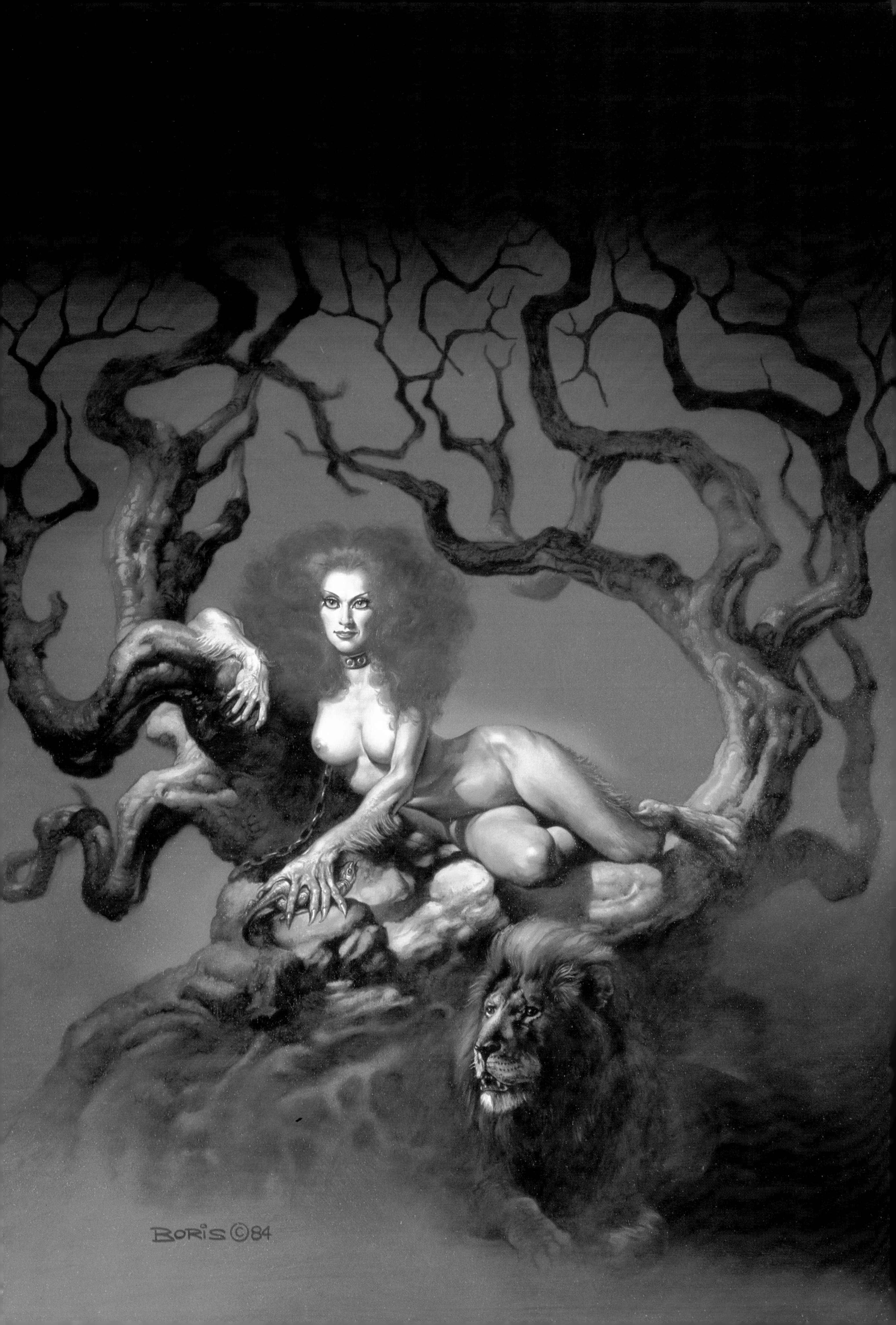
BORIS ©84

she moved through the hoop too quickly to be burned.

He told her the more often she braved it, the faster her fear would diminish.

He told her the conquest of fear was the simplest thing in the world: she need only pretend to be fearless.

The Sphinx yawns and stretches in her thirty-foot cage, which has been decorated with plastic bulrushes, grasses, and a dead tree refurbished with plastic foliage. She shakes her red hair back from her face and is immediately aware that the Lion who sometimes shares this cage is also awake.

She'd been sleeping, her dreams filled with pictures of a road to the ancient city of Thebes, of another Sphinx and of an Oedipus she never knew. The dream Sphinx had just murdered an army of men. Blood spiraled from their corpses like red ticker tape, creating the trappings of a parade or a political rally. The dream Oedipus was as handsome as a fairytale prince. He spoke most poignantly of his love for the Sphinx. But he had a way of making love to her that seemed almost brutal. He did not bite or strike her. She was not bruised or injured in any way. Yet his compelling weight, his mouth, his strong hands tightening on her breasts caused the flutterings of an exquisite terror to throb in her veins.

She is aware of the Lion watching her although he affects an air of disinterest. She stretches again, rises, saunters toward him, flicks her tail in his face as she passes, and returns to her spot. She lies down, curls up, reaches between her legs with her rose petal tongue and begins to lick her sex.

The Lion, his dark muzzle wrinkling, lifts his head to inhale her scent. She stops what she is doing, rises, approaches him again, rubs her shoulders and flanks against his chest, and retreats. This time he follows

her. At her spot she crouches down on all fours, her tail trembling.

The Lion sniffs her rump and then nuzzles her. She skips away and he follows. She circles him, dancing up to brush against him and leaping away until, finally, he catches her from behind. His mouth closes gently on the back of her neck, his powerful forepaws are planted on either side of her, his hindquarters thrust against her slowly, almost casually at first, then with increasing urgency.

When he releases her, she rolls over on her back and he lies down next to her. It is then that she notices the Lion Trainer standing outside the cage looking at them. She closes her eyes, not to shut him out but to read his scent, his breathing, the shifting slipstream of his thoughts. When she opens her eyes, he is gone.

She refuses to jump through the flaming hoop at the matinee performance.

He cracks the whip once, twice, three times, four times.

She turns her back on him and stares out at the audience.

He comes up behind her in order to touch her with the whip. She flicks her tail in his face and bounds

away. As if the ensuing jeers were bloody meat, they quiet an ache in her belly.

The evening performance, which the Lion Trainer dreads, goes like clockwork.

When the Sphinx is down on all fours, she is no taller than the Midget. They stand eye to eye, a fact that holds great attraction for him. From their mutual point of view, the horizon is much higher than for others; for no one else does the earth have to stretch so far to reach the sky.

The Midget is twenty-five years old, thirty-five inches high, and humiliatingly dependent on others. He can't walk down the street alone lest he be harrassed or injured. He must be lifted into and out of chairs, propped up on telephone books to see across ordinary tables. He has to be lifted in and out of his own van even though it has his name emblazoned in gold letters on both sides.

Worst of all is the unshakable notion that all this is his fault. Logically, he knows, it is not. Still, his guilt is confirmed in the looks others give him and in their attitudes toward him. There are no other midgets in his family. His parents, tall and beautiful, are aerialists. Since childhood he dreamed of joining their act. He imagined himself, resplendent in white tights, sailing across the top of the circus tent like a shooting star.

"Midgets don't fly," his parents told him.

He wanted to anyway.

"Be grateful that you're the only midget in the circus," they said. "Competition is cutthroat."

He felt like a mosquito they were trying to swat. Even so, he continued his entreaties against their indifference. One day his father allowed him to climb to a platform some fifty feet above the ground. He positioned him on the swing and let him go. As the Midget arched high over the heads of those below, the rope suddenly broke. He plummeted heavily to the safety net, which he struck face down, from which he bounced and rebounded, and in which he at last lay still. Thus he understood, to his enduring disgust, that he was a coward; that, on the battlefield of his psyche, fear outweighed ambition.

His father lifted him triumphantly out of the net and asked him how he had liked his flight.

Wretched and defeated, the Midget wailed, "You cut the rope!"

"For your own good," his father said. "Because flying is dangerous and I'm thinking of your future."

Though the Midget suspected his father had other reasons, he never ventured up the ladder again. The closest he came to flying after that was being swung aloft in the rough embrace of an elephant's trunk. Often enough he wished the beast would drop him,

crush him in full view of the shrieking spectators so his father would regret his treachery.

Then a sphinx came to the circus, a sphinx with amber skin, oblique eyes, and furry haunches that ended in lethally clawed feet. The Lion Trainer never entered her cage without a long whip or a steel chair to keep her at a distance with. For this sheepish behavior he was considered brave and the gallery applauded.

One of the bars of her cage was bent just enough for the Midget to squeeze through. Were he to do that, he would not bring a whip; he would not bring a weapon of any kind. He would offer her his trust —should he enter the cage.

Should he?

Shouldn't he?

The process of falling in love was swift and bedazzling. From one minute to the next his blood swelled, his heart grew stronger, worn-out landscapes were suddenly vibrant with color, extinguished dreams once again surged with life: midgets were no less in stature than giants.

And if she had no use for his trust?

But the lover is special and cannot be shackled by earthbound considerations.

The Sphinx is flattered by his attention. His stories make the time pass. Before he came to entertain her, the long days drifted endlessly. He is the only midget she has ever met. Although he is an adult, he has the voice of a child. Or, more precisely, the voice of a toy. She finds his passion for flying as well as his longings for death incongruous with his appearance; indeed, rather laughable. She keeps this to herself, however. What she does express is her curiosity to see what he looks like under his little plaid flannel shirt and his tiny denims.

He is hesitant about showing her. This is, he uneasily confesses (after her persistent queries), because he is afraid she will be disappointed. His penis, though certainly proportionate with his size, is so much smaller than those of other men.

Her vulva, she tells him, bears no resemblance to those of other women. Yet, far from being self-conscious about it, she feels that it rather suits her. She has, in fact, been told how beautiful it is by more than one lover. To illustrate this, she rolls on her back and displays it to him.

He examines it, touches it delicately, smells it, and determines that it has a surprisingly piquant taste reminiscent of caramels dipped in brine. He allows her to undress him, to play with him, lick him, stroke him. He is amazed at her gentleness. Having imagined lovemaking with her to be a desperate, life-threatening act—the cleaving of two very alien species—he is simultaneously relieved and troubled. Does she think he is too fragile? Too weak? Is her tenderness nothing but caution?

"I think it's outrageous that you have to share this place with a lion," he says after they have been lovers for a week and a half.

"He's only here on matinee days," she says. "Something to do with union regulations. Merely convenience."

"It's an indignity that you should object to on principle alone, if for no other reason."

The Sphinx closes her eyes.

"If you give people a hand, the next thing you know is they've ripped off an arm. And by that I mean, if you don't object to a lion they're likely to start housing the orangutans in here next."

She laughs. As far as she is concerned, the orangutans are welcome.

The Midget interprets this as a form of repulse. He stays away for three days during which he decides that she is more beast than human; during which he tells himself that he is well rid of her; during which he thinks of her constantly; during which it seems he will go mad thinking of her: the more he banishes her from his mind, the more forcefully she returns. At the end of three days he reappears at her cage and informs her that he doesn't want her making love to lions, to orangutans, or to other men. Nor does he want her dreaming of them.

"And why in the world should I limit myself?" she asks, somewhat irked by this aggressiveness that shows a side of him she has not known.

"Because I dream only of you," he says. "Because I love only you."

She turns from him, leaps onto the dead tree, and stretches out on one of its thick, gnarled branches. A full two minutes pass before she speaks. "You are very sweet most of the time. And you tell very interesting stories. We laugh a lot when we're together, which is very nice. I do love you, you know. But I'm not in love with you."

"Why not? You admit that you like my stories and I'm sweet and nice. What else do I have to be for you to be in love with me?"

"You would have to be bigger," she says, her tail slapping the branch loudly.

"As big as the Lion Trainer, I suppose?"

"As big as an elephant."

The Midget's face goes quite red. "You're not by any chance telling me, are you, that you could fall in love with an elephant?"

"Yes," she says simply.

"Do you know any elephants? First hand, I mean?"

She shakes her head.

"Well," the Midget pauses dramatically and then shifts into high gear, "you wouldn't like them. To begin with,

they're overly temperamental. Unlike midgets, they won't tolerate pushing around. Of course you may think that I'm prejudiced, that I'm saying these things out of jealousy or whatever. But a playful swipe from an elephant's trunk can break your arm. And if you want to be nice to them, if you bring them carrots or peanuts or banana peels, they'll eat out of your hand to start with, all right, and then they'll grab you and knock you off your feet to get more."

The Sphinx's eyes glint wickedly. "It's not my feet that need knocking."

The Midget draws himself up a full half inch more. "If it's genital size you're interested in, I can tell you that the male elephant's penis gets as long and as thick as a weightlifter's arm. However, I feel it's only fair to add that he uses it primarily to scratch his stomach. This leaves the female elephants rather dependent on their trainer for fun. He obliges by telling them dirty jokes and scratching them behind the ears. If that's what you want, then of course, by all means, get yourself an elephant."

"It's hard to believe you're not prejudiced," The Sphinx remarks.

When she was very young, the Sphinx once saw a man mauled by a lion. Not long afterward, she saw two lions mating. These events struck her as having many similarities.

Being a hybrid, she was not restricted to any one species in the selection of a lover. What she wanted was something more than what she'd witnessed either between the two lions or between the lion and the man. Since she had such a wide range of creatures to choose from, there was no reason to suppose she would not find the right one. She longed for tenderness and for the profound, fierce intimacy of a lifelong bonding.

She was familiar with the legends of her ancestor who had waylaid and killed so many men. What she missed in these legends were the causes to account for these grisly effects. Had the men, seeing a sphinx on their road, approached her with threats? Had they laughed at her questions? Had they been stupid beyond endurance? She did not know any men at the time and thus reached no conclusions. It was only much later on that she found a quasi answer in the paradoxical axiom: one generally gets what one wants out of life, but not what one dreams of.

Her first lover was a fox. His red coat was the color of her own long hair. She loved his pointy, sensitive little ears, which could hear things hers could not: a rabbit in the underbrush, the movements of a snake, emerald green lizards scampering to the camouflage of grass, the silvery rain pattering on distant leaves.

And she loved his moist little nose, which could detect the hours-old passage of a field mouse, the presence of a hungry predator, the soundless approach of winter. In embracing him she hoped to embrace a world that had largely, until then, eluded her.

The Fox, lavish and tender with his caresses, was as gentle a lover as she had wished for. His teasing and fondling put her in a kind of trance. She hardly felt him enter her. She was dreaming that he was not a fox at all but a male sphinx, his body sculpted gold, his paws richly padded velvet. When the pain of the Fox's thrusts registered, she reacted with a startled jerking away and knocked him to the ground. He leaped up with a cry. As she only glared at him accusingly, he ran off. She never saw him again, which made her realize what enormous power lovers had to wound each other. She resolved to keep the lesson in mind for the future: to listen more closely to the language of the senses and not to mistake silence for an absence of need. As she fell in and out of love during the subsequent years, however, she forgot again and again.

Not long after the Fox left her, she fell in love with a Unicorn. Since she'd heard that unicorns were mythological beasts and did not exist in real life, she considered herself extraordinarily lucky to have found him. All the same, his behavior did not jibe with her expectations.

He was boisterous, opinionated, and egocentric. He never consulted her on anything, never inquired about her feelings, never asked her opinion. If, on occasion, she expressed an idea that conflicted with any of his, he would launch into a strident, pauseless monologue that, steamroller fashion, annihilated it.

Convinced that these rough edges of his would slough off as long as she remained patient and understanding, she stored all his sins in her heart while she dismissed them in her head. She made lists of all his good qualities. He was elegant, long-legged, strong. He was intelligent, warm, gregarious, generous. He had a good sense of humor. His athletic talents were impressive. He could clear obstacles well over ten feet high. His full gallop closely approached the speed of sound. He was resourceful in his lovemaking, though this, in a way, led finally to their parting.

They had attended a moonlight bacchanal. He enjoyed himself unrestrainedly, as usual, dancing more wildly than anyone else and laughing more loudly. Also as usual, she remained primarily an observer. At the height of the bedlam and drunkenness, he drew much attention by demonstrating a dancing trot, a trot in place (both of which he claimed to have picked up at the Spanish Riding School of Vienna), a canter on three legs, a backwards canter, and, finally, a canter pirouette done while balancing an obscenely grinning young faun on the tip of his single horn. On all this she merely commented that it was nice to see him having a good time.

Perhaps inspired by the cheers and encouragement he received for his stunt with the faun, he suggested the following day, as he was warming up for a morning-after fuck, that he use his horn for the purpose. She listened quietly to his suggestion and, by her docile manner, seemed to be in agreement. As he lowered his head and leveled his horn at her, however, she leaped onto his back and clawed him so viciously he almost died from loss of blood.

In recent years she has begun to feel that the distinction between love and hate is diminishing. She believes that she loves the Lion Trainer and yet she can delight in humiliating him by being intractable during a performance, by baring her teeth at him, by unsheathing her claws, or by ignoring him altogether. Conversely, she may be longing to tear great, angry wounds in his flesh and will, instead, roll onto her back when he approaches and purr with happiness when he strokes her smooth belly.

At times she wishes for the life she would have had if she'd remained in the wilderness. Though with the circus she travels widely and the settings of her life are always changing, the content of her days seldom varies. How would things be if she had never met the Lion Trainer? This wistful inquiry, never addressed to anyone in particular, is never answered.

It seems to her that the Lion Trainer, too, must have his unanswered questions. One day she overhears him say to a clown: "From the time you're born you're taught to believe that life follows a rational pattern; that you will grow up, get wiser, know right from wrong, be rewarded if you follow the golden rules and live happily ever after. By the time you reach thirty, you've come to realize that these are all lies."

THIRST

What does the moon-haunted night whisper to leaves to make them turn yellow and fall? What does it call across desolate landscapes? What does it wail at mutely listening tombstones?

The worst thing is to know too exactly. To feel the changes too exactly: the alien painlessness invading the body like frost, penetrating the flesh to the bone marrow.

To see too exactly through fixed and staring eyes how, in the tight space of a coffin, the dark is packed around one's body. To understand, incontrovertibly, that since one can see every corner, every black shape in this profound blackness, the nightmare so willingly entered is real. It was naive to suppose that any death and rebirth could be devoid of terror.

Once, a very long time ago, I discovered the bleached and perfect skeleton of a seagull lying on a beach. The scavengers that always feed on dead things had rejected this corpse as, now, they do mine. I remember wondering, at the time, what mortal sin this seagull could possibly have committed. Several white feathers still clung to the hollow bones as if with the heroic tenacity of life.

It is with the same tenacity that my *humanness* clings to me. When it is finally gone, according to B (the vampire whose contagious thirst turned me into a vampire), all ambivalence and guilt will be gone along with it. Meanwhile the sunrises that beckon to me with death remain a poignant memory of the time when I was still alive.

I could make a thousand excuses for having become what I am. I could say that I was deluded, bewitched, unaware of what I was actually doing, incapable of an untainted choice.

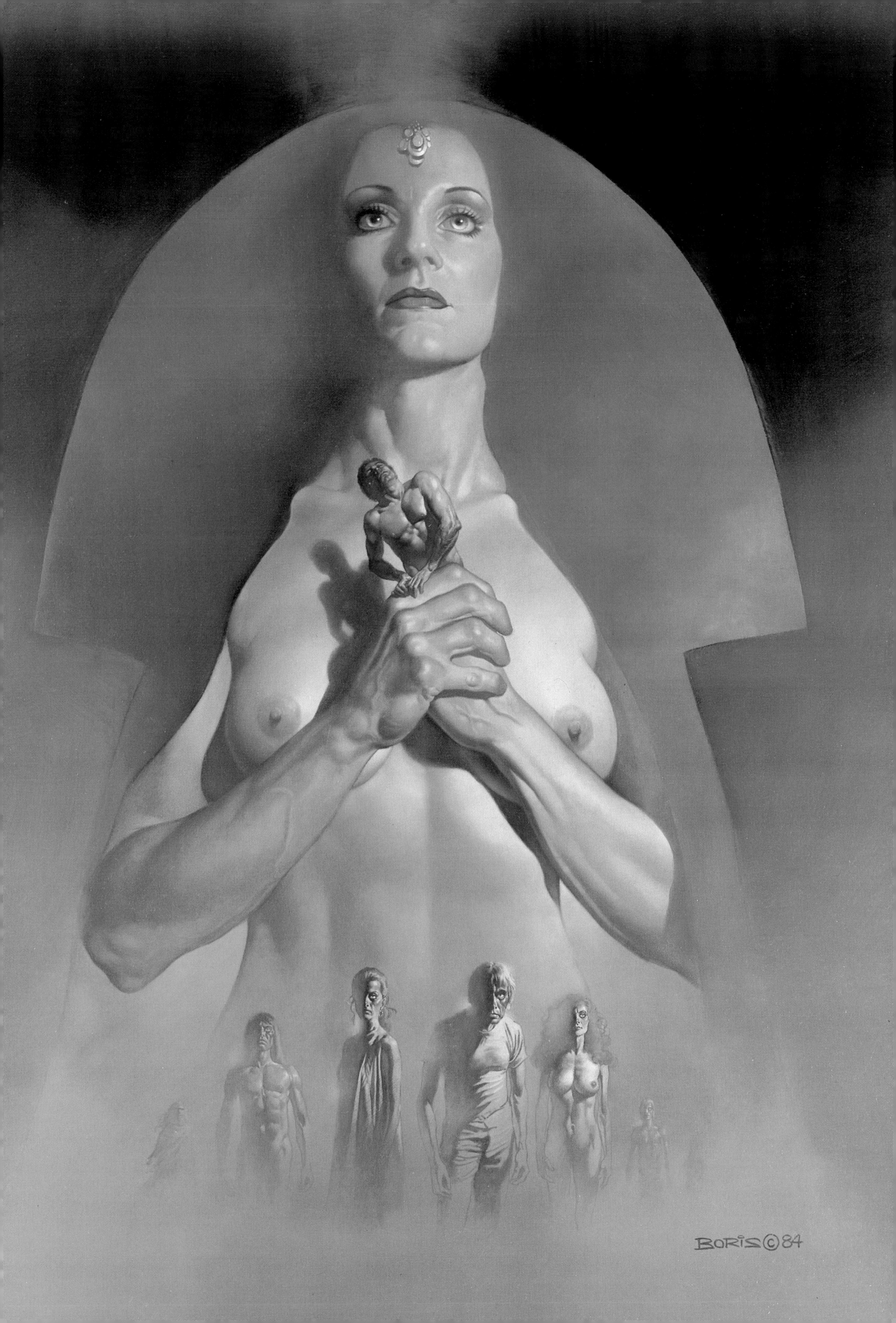
BORIS©84

I could describe how he first appeared, how he materialized, magnificent and terror-breathing, out of the velvet depths of a thicket on the night when, unable to sleep, I had gone walking alone in the park, half wishing for some misadventure.

I could tell how, even before I saw him, I was aware of the nearness of some exceptional being, how I heard (or thought I heard) the drumbeat of invisible wings match the suddenly furious pounding of my own anxious heart.

I could describe the abrupt silence that accompanied his appearance: the chirruping night sounds sharply stilled, the sound of my own breathing cut short, the movement of shadows frozen, even the far-off clouds halted in their meandering drift across the moon. I could describe the radiance of his pale skin that might itself have been made of clouds shot with moonlight. His black hair. His green eyes. His finely shaped mouth, rendered eerily sensual by the pearly hint of fangs—so tantalizing a suggestion of danger. I could plead the weakness that flooded my body at his approach, leaving me unable to avert my eyes.

And his hands on my bare skin, the confidence of his icy caresses that conjured such heat, such a frenzy out of me. I could describe how his lovemaking sank me down into cradling darkness and robbed me of all past and future until the fierce, sweet, murderous thrust of his fangs buoyed me up again, crazily up with a drunken exhilarating sensation of flight.

But what difference would a long catalog of excuses make? The truth is that I agreed to be killed by a vampire in order to become a vampire and live forever. My agreement introduces the question of guilt. But the truth is also that I might have become a vampire with or without my agreement, and too often the mere obvious passes as truth, thus cloaking many secrets beneath its surface.

Furthermore, the truth can change in no time at all. In a matter of hours it can attain a wholly different shading. It can become a non-truth. It can become a consummate lie.

What I have come to understand is this: that it will not help to hold B responsible for my unslakable thirst and growing despair.

Those whose dreams can be measured in centimeters will condemn me outright, I know. It's not to them, unresistant as slaughter-bound sheep, that I appeal for understanding. They accept the extinguishing of a consciousness as benignly as the turning off of a light. Let them prate their smug morality and condone their God's mysterious ways. What can they understand about the temptation of the dream, those who have never been blinded by its dazzling madness, who have never considered the implications of no longer being, of leaving their loves, of vanishing—of all their memories and wishes vanishing. What can I say to people who quiescently resign themselves to such losses?

Becoming a vampire did not seem tantamount to making a pact with the Devil. In some ways it was more like falling in love. Especially at the beginning as, night by night, the earth grew more beautiful. And I, an ever more sensate creature, grew aware of such things as caterpillars changing to moths in their silky wombs, of the faintest of exotic scents on the wind, and of the distant worlds of silvery fire anchoring each shaft of starlight.

At the beginning each sunset delivered the earth to me in richer, more beguiling colors. It was a superb adventure, all the more so because each beginning was no longer trailed by its inevitable end and there was nothing I had to mourn in advance. Each evening I gave myself to this adventure like a woman unreservedly opening herself to her beloved; every glance, every touch of his precious to her. Every caress treasured. Even the pain he inflicts on her treasured because it comes from him.

I was slow to realize that killing caused me pain. For close to a century it was inseparable from pleasure. To kill is as instinctive for a neophyte vampire as sucking is for a human infant. Selectivity and discretion are learned in time. I was, in a sense, an infant those first hundred years.

Not that I ambushed my prey like a thief or struck only the helpless. I hunted in the most civilized of settings: parties, political rallies, theater lobbies. I usually courted my victims, cultivated their friendships first. Ultimately I gave them, I felt, more than I took. Who, after all, would not prefer the immortality I had to offer over a few mean decades of ordinary life? I was so certain of the answer.

This certainty ended abruptly around the middle of my second hundred years.

"I think it might be better not to," my new conquest said. I was undoing the buttons of his shirt. "It's distracting with all these people just outside. You never know when someone will take it into his head to barge in."

The occasion was his farewell party. He was planning to leave for the coast on the following day.

"I want the last time to be good," he said. "And these circumstances are hardly ideal."

I slipped my hands into his open shirt. The laughter, the babble of voices, the ice clinking in glasses throughout the rest of the house made the bedroom hushed and intimate by contrast. I undid his pants. I felt him

harden. I half hoped he would grab me roughly and make swift, brutal love to me, to which the kill would come as a perfect climax. But he was clearly distracted by the sounds of the party. I opened my gown, lay down on the bed, and drew him on top of me. For the smallest moment his apprehension gripped me too and I almost said, "Yes, let's forget it. This is not a good time." Then I warmed to the feel of this naked man, to his smell, to the blood pounding in his neck, so close to my lips. And I slipped beyond thought to the voluptuous joy of pure sensation.

It was over quickly enough, but not before the shouting and the door crashing open tore me back to reality. Escaping through the open window, I cast one last look at my dead lover collapsed on the rumpled bed, at his young, firm-fleshed body that would, thanks to me, never grow old.

His left arm, bent at the elbow, encircled his head. And the right one was flung outward, palm up, as if entreating me to stay. Yet the expression on his face was unrelated to that gesture. His open mouth framed a curse frozen into silence. Anger glittered in his shock-glazed eyes. The blood draining from the wound in his neck was a denunciation. And the sight of it struck a sudden deep pain into me.

I don't know when, exactly, the others began to despise me, to align themselves against me. My first awareness of their hostility was bewildering. I felt no corresponding hatred for B. I decided that the newness of being immortal must have worn off and they were looking for something to replace it. And, I told myself, because they didn't actually know what that something was, they settled for revenge. They disregarded the uniqueness of their situation for the cheap, banal comfort of revenge. Their existences, which might still have been fascinating enough, had narrowed to suit their myopia.

I understood that they planned to destroy me. Thus I arose every evening as soon as the last sanguine ray of the sun had seeped from the sky. There was no way for them to reach me before that. And after that I was invulnerable.

Yet their relentless hatred contaminates me. It makes me wonder (inevitably, I suppose) if it might not have been better to remain human after all, to have retained that frailty, that relative innocence that a temporal existence implies. Unwilling to accept this, however, I tracked down B (who I hadn't seen in years) to ask his opinion.

As awed as my first impression of him had been —the luminous skin, the hypnotic eyes—I now realize that these adjectives might describe any vampire.

Passing centuries and the diet of human blood gives us all the same abnormally whitened skin, the same hectic touch of color in the cheeks after we've drunk, the same dry, staring eyes.

Perhaps because he was the first vampire I ever knew, I always thought he was different from the others, remote and mysterious. I thought the grief reflected in his handsome features had nothing to do with human grief, that it beat inside him like a beautiful inhuman heart and magically drew him to me. Only now I see it was the beat of his thirst that drew him, that unfolded within him like an evil flower, inuring him to violence and to hope.

What ineffable solace I once found in his arms when, like great soft wings, they locked me to him. What refuge in his cool body, alive as the night. Once we were bound as no mortals ever could be. Once we were glorious midnight birds ascending toward midnight horizons on each other's wings.

I tracked him to his moldering tomb in the cellar of a neglected mansion. I greeted him. He neither stirred nor answered but lay in his coffin like a drowned thing at the bottom of the sea. It was only after the moon had gone down and the stars burned with renewed and ominous brilliance that I succeeded in rousing him. He was not interested in philosophizing at that point and wanted only to go on the hunt.

The man began to die even before B touched him. You could see it in his pallor, in the helpless gaping O of his mouth, in his trembling, already cadaverish body. He was lying on a park bench, a newspaper spread across his arms and chest for protection against the cold.

A hundred feet off someone had started a fire in a trash basket and was warming himself. The wind blew smoke in our direction. The air was acrid with the smell of burning trash. Naturally we were impervious to it. But our victim's eyes, red-rimmed and rheumy, overflowed with tears. He could not have known what we were. Human beings in this age don't believe in vampires. And yet he began to struggle, to gasp for the smoke-putrid air, his body already stricken, already cowering before a fate his dimming brain could hardly understand.

He was so close to death by the time B, bending over him, inhaled his wind-sodden breath, that killing him might have seemed merciful. But B tore such a hole in his throat the sudden gush of blood was more than he could drink at once. In an instant the man's neck, the bench on which he lay, and the ground beneath bloomed an awful red. The blood burst from him with such strength, such fury. I knelt beside them and it pumped over my hands. Though blood is hardly

repugnant to me, I was shaken by the unexpected sight of it on me, by the doomed throb of it on my hands.

I shouted at B to stop. I tried to pull him away. I struck at him with clenched fists, splashing his clothes with blood. Fastened on the dying man, he unselfconsciously drank like a pig—this malignant shadow, this castrated god, this lord of nothingness.

I ran.

Buildings and cars snapped past me. People and lights streamed by.

I stopped on a deserted street and vomited my poisoned dream.

I longed for death.

A figure appeared at the end of the block. A shadow (no more real than myself) with an incandescent face, dead as the moon: the man whose dying I had run from. How had he risen already? How had he gotten here so soon? I wanted to tell him that I had tried to save his life. But this matchstick construction of words collapsed on my tongue.

More vampires gathered, silent as memories. A ghostly lynch mob, they skulked in doorways, they glowed in the blank eyes of windows, they crowded the street. I remembered them, each of them one night older than the next. And I remembered how selfishly I had loved them.

Their mouths stained black with old blood, incessant thirst etching their faces, they lie in wait for me like nightmares at the edge of sleep. Wherever I go, they stalk me. Sometimes one or another or several of them glide up to me. They never actually touch me. But the nightmare intensifies. They are the witnesses against me, the evidence of all my transgressions. And, despite my remorse, their number grows.

It must stop, I tell myself. Or one night we will outnumber the living. One night there will be no living left. If insanity offered a refuge from this future, I would gladly go insane. But it does not. If it would at least throw them off my track I would go insane. It does not do that, either. So, hiding from the sun, I pray for the sun to find me; I pray for it to find all of us. I pray for its freeing, purifying light.

I still remember a sunrise I observed more than two hundred years ago. The memory of it has that peculiar quality of seeming to belong to someone else. As though it had been transplanted into my brain. I remember the exquisite red of it slowly staining the morning sky. I thought that red was the blood of God before I realized that his blood, chameleonlike, was colorless. It must therefore be the blood of the night that the sun, in its waking ritual, had murdered. Did some element of precognition instill in me, so very long ago, my chastening deference for the sun?

Now that I am chained to an unpardoning eternity, it seems a luxury to die unjudged, as the night dies.

What is it that men, embarked on a gory mission, whisper to each other in stricken voices? What god do they pray to in their unholy anguish? What unuttered howls are pumped to their brains by their violently hammering hearts?

The worst thing is to know too exactly. To hear their soft approach too clearly. To sense too keenly which of them grips the wooden stake in his sweat-frozen hand. To see his face too distinctly through the opaque coffin lid, the frightful intensity of that face: the eyes unnaturally wide and close to bursting from his head; the sickly sheen glazing his skin; the hair rising in high, jagged relief, giving the impression of black flames.

The worst thing is to know in advance how, for a single heinous instant, we will be linked by a common terror: by the nerve-rending crash of the coffin thrown too vehemently open. And by the stupefying shock of this confrontation, the irony of it: murderer vis-à-vis murderess.

I know the sounds and sights as if by heart: the short, strangled intake of breath; the stake descending in a lightning arc, hard and white-hot as my first inhuman lover's kiss; my own cry as it pierces my delirious heart. And the crescendoing echoes of that cry as I rise, mistlike, from my crumbling corpse. I know, as if by heart, how my wings will unfold to take me up through the shattering echoes, a nightbird, invisible against the sky.

ABOUT THE AUTHOR AND THE ILLUSTRATOR

Doris Vallejo, a native New Yorker, was a successful illustrator before turning to writing. Her publications include a children's book, *The Boy Who Saved the Stars*, and a science fiction novel, *Windsound*. She wrote the text for *Mirage*.

Born in Lima, Peru, Boris Vallejo is one of America's foremost fantasy illustrators. He has gained worldwide attention for his stunning illustrations of science fiction and fantasy; his works appear on the covers of books by such writers as Edgar Rice Burroughs, Alice Chetwynd Ley, Frederik Pohl, Larry Niven, and Lin Carter, as well as in such well-known series as Doc Savage, Tarzan, and Conan. Much of his art was published in *The Fantastic Art of Boris Vallejo*. He also created the illustrations for *Mirage*.

Doris and Boris make their home in New Jersey.